HOW to GET $100,000 WORTH OF SERVICES
FREE
EACH YEAR from the UNITED STATES GOVERNMENT

HOW TO GET $100,000 WORTH OF SERVICES *FREE*, EACH YEAR, FROM THE U.S. GOVERNMENT

By E. Joseph Cossman

A World of Books That Fill a Need

Frederick Fell Publishers, Inc. New York

From time to time the author, E. Joseph Cossman, gives business seminars across the country. If you'd like to know when a seminar will be given in your city, you can get this information by writing to:

Mr. E. Joseph Cossman
P.O. Box 1066
Studio City, Calif. 91604

Library of Congress Cataloging in Publication Data

Cossman, E   Joseph.
    How to get $100,000 worth of services free, each year, from the U. S. Government.

    Editions of 1965 and 1969 published under title: How to get $50,000 worth of services free, each year, from the U.S. Government.
        1. Business—Information services. 2. Industry and state—United States. I. Title.
HF5353.C7 1975   353   75-13973
ISBN 0-8119-0257-9

Cl 10.78

For information address:
Frederick Fell Publishers, Inc.
386 Park Avenue South
New York, N.Y. 10016
Published simultaneously in Canada by
George J. McLeod, Limited, Toronto 2B, Ontario
MANUFACTURED IN THE UNITED STATES OF AMERICA

Dedicated to My Father,

THEODORE H. COSSMAN

WHO, LIKE THOUSANDS OF OTHERS,
HAD THE COURAGE AND FORESIGHT TO LEAVE HIS NATIVE
LAND
SO HIS CHILDREN COULD BE BORN AND RAISED
IN THIS WONDERFUL, WONDERFUL COUNTRY.

EDITOR'S NOTE

While the author has attempted to be as current and as accurate as possible with subscription prices and fees, we are unable to guarantee that prices will remain the same. If there is any doubt, please contact the appropriate party directly. All prices are subject to change without notice.

TABLE OF CONTENTS

8

HOW to GET $100,000 WORTH OF SERVICES
FREE
EACH YEAR from the UNITED STATES GOVERNMENT

INTRODUCTION

A harassed farmer sat down one day and penned a letter:

"DEAR GOVERNMENT: Will you please tell me how to get rid of dandelions? I've tried everything."

Eventually he got his answer:

"DEAR SIR: We don't know of anything that will get rid of dandelions, but here's a great recipe for dandelion wine."

While Abraham Lincoln was still delivering the mail in his stovepipe hat, citizens were turning to Uncle Sam with their problems. Then, as now, Uncle was ready to help out, if he could; and if he couldn't, he could always suggest dandelion wine. When the mail got too heavy to answer in the friendly fashion above, form letters were substituted; and finally the present practice evolved of issuing publications on every subject an American citizen might be interested in.

Housewife, mariner, trout fisherman, or astronaut; chess player, rock hound, farmer, or mortician: whatever your interest, your Uncle Sam has valuable help and information for you. Much of it is yours for the asking. The rest is offered well under cost. The information in one publication alone, *General, Social and Economics, U. S. Summary* is yours for $2.25. Much of what you'll find in it is unavailable anywhere else.

Uncle Sam runs the largest publishing house in the world just for you. Created in 1860, the Government Printing Office turns out a staggering amount of material every year. There are over 1,250,000 titles in print, and more are pouring out at the rate of 20,000 annually.

All the material is carefully prepared by recognized experts in the field. It is as accurate, factual, and helpful as is humanly possible to make it.

Want to go into a new business? What are your chances for success? What's the best location? How much money do you need? The best stock to buy? You have a thousand such questions on your minds. To whom will you turn for help? You can't always trust suppliers, for they're eager to sell you their goods. You can't always trust real-estate agents, for they're anxious to rent you their property. You can't always trust your friends, for they are bent upon giving you sugar-coated advice just to keep you happy. And you certainly can't trust your competitors, for many of them would do anything to keep you out of business.

But Uncle Sam has nothing to sell you but help. He has no ax to grind, and his information is impartial and objective.

Looking for a new product to sell? Uncle Sam will tell you how to develop new products and give you lists of royalty-free inventions from which you may choose. (See Chapter III.)

Interested in running a business out of your own home? He's ready to help with solid, valuable information. (See Chapter I.)

Want to sell overseas? The Bureau of International Commerce will actually locate jobbers, dealers, agents for you in any country you can name. (See Chapter IV.)

Want to learn a language? The government offers

manuals not only on French, Spanish, Italian, or German, but on Swahili, Urdu, Hindi! (See Chapter IX.)

Got an inventive mind? The role of the Patent Office is well known, but are you aware that the Department of Commerce publishes lists of inventions wanted by the Armed Forces and other government agencies? (See Chapter VI.)

Got something to sell? Uncle Sam can be your best customer. Moreover, the government issues regular lists of products wanted and continually solicits bids. Those lists are yours for the asking. (See Chapter VI.)

Got an idea that has commercial possibilities for some industry, yet can't be patented or copyrighted? How do you protect yourself? A lawyer's advice will cost you $50 or $100. The Government furnishes, free, Small Business Management Aid No. 53, *Small Business Profits from Unpatentable Ideas* which, among other valuable information, gives you rules for protecting an intangible but saleable idea. (See Chapter V.)

Would you like Uncle Sam to grubstake you for a prospecting expedition? He'll do it! (See Chapter V.)

Want to know how to keep from losing your shirt in mail order? Ask Uncle. (See Chapter I.)

Ever dream of living on a lazy Bali H'ai type island of your own in the South Seas? Uncle will sell you one . . . cheap! (See Chapter V.)

Cutthroat competition getting you down? You don't have to go under. (See Chapter II.)

Would you like the President of General Motors to represent your company abroad . . . at no charge? It could happen, if you asked for Uncle's free help from the right trade mission. (See Chapter IV.)

Like to bring customers into your store with a free movie every day? Uncle Sam shows you where to find them. (See Chapter V.)

Want to get the "red carpet" treatment when you travel to Europe . . . at no extra charge? It happened to me; it could happen to you! (See Chapter IV.)

Need art work or photographs for your advertising? The Library of Congress and the National Archives have probably ten million pictures on file. Virtually all Government agencies and departments in Washington take pictures of their activities and projects, whether it be building roads, counting fish, or firing earth satellites into space. They keep files of these and fill photo requests at very low prices. (See Chapter IX.)

Is foreign competition infringing on your trade-mark or copyright? You may call on the Treasury Department of the United States to prohibit the entry of such infringing foreign-made merchandise into this country. (See Chapter VIII.)

All right. What you've just read only scratches the surface of what your government is anxious to give to you for little or nothing. Nobody could tell it all. Even the government itself can't keep track of the flood of valuable and useful information and knowledge that spews out yearly from the Government Printing Office. The various government agencies try to keep on top of the flood with their own compiled lists, but it's almost impossible. However, because of the multitude of information that is gathered each day by the Government, it's safe to assume as a working rule:

IF THERE'S ANYTHING YOU WANT TO KNOW
ABOUT ANYTHING UNDER THE SUN, YOUR
GOVERNMENT PROBABLY HAS A PAMPHLET
ON IT!

These publications range from a single-page handout to a monthly volume which in itself is a bibliography of government publications, entitled, *Monthly Catalog of U. S. Govern-*

INTRODUCTION 15

ment Publications, available by subscription from the Government Printing Office.

Does the public use this tremendous wealth of material? Well, the largest selling book in the history of the United States is the government's brochure on *Infant Care.* It outsells the Bible. Eight and a half million copies have been distributed . . . so far.

A tremendous achievement? Perhaps. But when you consider that there are fifty million *mothers* in this country it becomes evident that the people who *don't* know how to use the government's resources far outnumber those who *do!*

The situation in relation to business is even worse. A dozen government agencies put out information vital to businessmen. That's where this book comes in. The volume you hold in your hand is unique. It pulls together all the *best* material from all agencies and sources for one purpose: to show the businessman the best that Uncle Sam has to offer him from every source. It gives you the big picture.

The purpose of this book is to acquaint you with the phenomenal variety, diversity, scope, and sheer *money value* that your Uncle Sam is begging you, as a consumer or as a businessman, to take advantage of. This book does not pretend to give an exhaustive list of the thousands of government resources at your fingertips for the asking, but it acts as a guide in directing you to these resources.

In addition to the publications, the pictures, the motion pictures (yes, the government agencies even have films on their activities which are available for your use), you will also learn of the services you can call upon for your own use as a citizen of the United States.

So you see, the title of this book is no exaggeration. As an American citizen, you *can* get $100,000 worth of business services *free* each year.

Your government *wants* you to take advantage of these

services. This book tells you how and where to obtain them.
The money you invested in this book is like taking a flier on
an oil well . . . when you already know the gusher has come
in! All you have to do is cash in.

Go to it!

Technical inquiries will be answered by the author if sent to the
following address:

Mr. E. Joseph Cossman
Post Office Box 1066
Studio City, California, 91604

CHAPTER I

UNCLE SAM AS YOUR BUSINESS PARTNER

STARTING YOUR OWN BUSINESS
WITH GOVERNMENT HELP

SO YOU WANT TO GO INTO BUSINESS!

While the notion is still a gleam in your eye, you've already got yourself a partner: your Uncle Sam. He's a funny partner in some ways.

If you're successful, he takes part of the profits through taxes. If you're *more* successful, he takes *more* of the profits.

If you go into the red, he *doesn't* pay half the debts. Through his Director of Internal Revenue, he will make some concessions. He'll allow you to offset your losses against your gains and forego some or all of his share of the profits. He'll even let you balance the bad years against the good years, with limitations. But fork over cash to pay your creditors? No, sir. Some partner!

All right, that's the bad part. Comes to about half a page. For the next two hundred pages or so, you're going to hear about the *other* side of that partner of yours, the *good* side. Nobody's perfect, but how's that for percentage?

UNCLE OPENS THE DOOR . . .

I've yet to meet any red-blooded, employed male in this country who hasn't at one time or another expressed a strong desire to be in business for himself. It's not a case of the grass looking greener; it's a normal tendency to resist authority and strive for independence.

If you've been contemplating starting a business of your own, either part or full time, Uncle Sam has a staff of experts who can save you (and help you make) thousands of dollars in time and sound advice. You couldn't afford to pay for even a small percentage of the man-hours that have gone into the research and development material which these experts have gathered to help you. Hundreds of booklets, pamphlets, brochures, books, and folders are available, and they're yours. All you have to do is ask for them.

Just one *free* bulletin might be the key which could open the door to an entirely new career for you.

THERE'S A GOLD MINE WAITING TO BE TAPPED . . .

This book wasn't written to encourage you to go into business for yourself. It wasn't published to tell you the occupation you should pursue. Its main purpose is to expose you to the many aids available to you as a taxpayer and also to the thousands of publications which the United States Government publishes each year—books and literature on file which can help you make money and save money. Many are free, some cost 25 cents, some 30 cents, others 45 cents or 60 cents or more. Regardless of the price, you'll be rewarded time and again for the modest initial investment you make.

This probably sounds as though I'm conducting a one man public-relations campaign for the Government Printing

Office. Actually, I am. From past experience, using the methods I've outlined in this book, I've had such great personal success in my business that I'd like to share them with others. I had to learn this information the hard way; all you have to do is follow a few simple instructions, and you'll have more material at your fingertips than you could gather in any other manner.

IT'S YOUR DECISION . . .

Let's say you agree with me that you want to go into business for yourself. Fine. But remember this truism because it's one of the most important suggestions I can give you:

Don't tell anyone at your present place of employment that you're thinking about opening your own shop, store, or business. It's really a personal matter: your own. Don't tell your friends. Word gets out, and the first thing you know you may be looking for a job months before you're ready to make the big plunge. Unless you are independently wealthy, it's sound advice to stay with one job until you are definitely set to move to another. This may sound elementary, but I've seen too many men with ideas which were nothing more than pipe dreams get kicked in the teeth because they were unprepared when they started "on their own."

EASY DOES IT . . .

Walk before you run. Find out all you can about the job opportunities in the business you have selected. Just remember, and take heart: probably nowhere else has Uncle knocked himself out more to help as much as he helps the businessman . . . you.

If this surprises you, if you haven't seen any of this help around, believe me, it's *your* fault, not his. Uncle Sam conducts the biggest printing plant in the world—the Government Printing Office—and from it he pours out floods of valuable material to assist you in every possible phase of your business life.

And right here I want to introduce you to a man who can become the greatest business contact you'll ever make. He's the man to see about the hundreds of government publications I'm going to tell you about in this book as well as the hundreds of thousands of other publications put out by the GPO. Whenever you're in doubt about how to get any of the books, magazines, leaflets, and booklets from any department of the government, you can write to: *Superintendent of Documents, U.S. Government Printing Office, Washington, D.C. 20402.* He'll have it, and he'll send it to you.

HELP IS ON THE WAY! . . .

A large proportion of the material is aimed at guiding you right from the very start of your business. The reason? Businesses fail. Failures are bad for the individual, for those around him, and for the country in general. Uncle *wants* you to succeed. And short of leading you by the hand through every step of the way, he's going to do what he can to put you into the happy roster of successful, profit-making businessmen.

YOUR FRIEND, THE DEPARTMENT OF COMMERCE . . .

Many departments and agencies of the government help the businessman, but the Department of Commerce (as you can tell from its name) is by far your best source of help in the business field. About half of the publications I'll be bringing to your attention in succeeding chapters come from that department. On the next page you'll see a list of the department's Field Offices. If one of them is near you, go in and get acquainted. I think your eyes will be opened.

Many of the publications you'll want will be available in the Field Office, so you can save time by asking there before you bother the busy Superintendent in Washington.

Also, certain libraries are designated as depositories for government publications. The Superintendent sends them all, or almost all, of the government publications as they come out. The list of the more than four hundred libraries is too long to give here, but if you ask for the *United States Department of Commerce Publications, Annual Supplement* (prices vary), you'll find the depository libraries listed. If one is in your city, you will be able to use it to save time and expense by borrowing or consulting the library's files.

Another name you're going to come across constantly in these pages is the Small Business Administration. The SBA is the first independent agency of the federal government ever established in peacetime solely to advise and assist the nation's small business concerns. This agency, too, has regional and branch offices throughout the country, so use the one nearest you to save time. The list is given below.

If you have occasion to go to Washington on business, make your first stop the department's headquarters at 14th and "E" streets. There's a Business Service Center there where a business analyst who knows his way around will direct you to the official and agency you'll need to see to complete your business quickly and properly.

Department of Commerce Field Offices

Alburquerque, New Mexico 87101
U.S. Courthouse
Area Code 505 Tel. 247–0311

Anchorage, Alaska 99501
306 Loussac-Sogn Building
Area Code 907 Tel. 272–6331

Atlanta, Georgia 30303
4th Floor Home Savings Building
75 Forsyth Street N.W.
Area Code 404 Tel. 526–6000

Baltimore, Maryland 20212
305 U.S. Customhouse
Gay and Lombard Streets
Area Code 301 Tel. 962–3560

Birmingham, Alabama 35205
Suite 200–201
908 S. 20th Street
Area Code 205 Tel. 325–3327

Boston, Massachusetts 02203
Room 510
John Fitzgerald Kennedy Federal
  Building
Area Code 617 Tel. 233–2312

Buffalo, New York 14203
504 Federal Building
117 Ellicott Street
Area Code 716 Tel. 842–3208

Charleston, South Carolina 29403
Federal Building, Suite 631
334 Meeting Street
Area Code 803 Tel. 577–4171

Charleston, West Virginia 25301
3002 New Federal Office Building
500 Quarrier Street
Area Code 304 Tel. 343–6196

Cheyenne, Wyoming 82001
6022 Federal Building
2120 Capitol Avenue
Area Code 307 Tel. 634–5920

Chicago, Illinois 60604
1486 New Federal Building
219 South Dearborn Street
Area Code 312 Tel. 353–4400

Cincinnati, Ohio 45202
8028 Federal Office Building
550 Main Street
Area Code 513 Tel. 684–2944

Cleveland, Ohio 44114
Room 600
666 Euclid Avenue
Area Code 216 Tel. 522–4750

Dallas, Texas 75202
Room 1200
1114 Commerce Street
Area Code 214 Tel. 749–3287

Denver, Colorado 80202
16419 Federal Building
20th and Stout Streets
Area Code 303 Tel. 297–3246

Des Moines, Iowa 50309
609 Federal Building
210 Walnut Street
Area Code 515 Tel. 284–4222

Detroit, Michigan 48226
445 Federal Building
Area Code 313 Tel. 226–6088

Greensboro, North Carolina 27402
258 Federal Building
W. Market Street
P.O. Box 1950
Area Code 919 Tel. 275–9111

Hartford, Connecticut 06103
18 Asylum Street
Area Code 203 Tel. 244–3530

Honolulu, Hawaii 96813
286 Alexander Young Building
1015 Bishop Street
Tel. 588–977

Houston, Texas 77002
5102 Federal Building
515 Rusk Avenue
Area Code 713 Tel. 228–0611

Jacksonville, Florida 32202
P.O. Box 35087
400 W. Bay Street
Area Code 904 Tel. 791–2796

Kansas City, Missouri 64106
Room 2011
911 Walnut Street
Area Code 816 Tel. 374–3141

Los Angeles, California 90015
Room 450
Western Pacific Building
1031 S. Broadway
Area Code 213 Tel. 688–2833

Memphis, Tennessee 38103
710 Home Federal Building
147 Jefferson Avenue
Area Code 901 Tel. 534–3214

Miami, Florida 33130
Room 821
City National Bank Building
25 W. Flagler Street
Area Code 305 Tel. 350–5267

Milwaukee, Wisconsin 53203
Straus Building
238 W. Wisconsin Avenue
Area Code 414 Tel. 272–8600

Minneapolis, Minnesota 55401
306 Federal Building
110 S. Fourth Street
Area Code 612 Tel. 334–2131

New Orleans, Louisiana 70130
909 Federal Office Building, S.,
610 South Street
Area Code 504 Tel. 527–6546

New York, New York 10007
41st Floor
Federal Office Building
26 Federal Plaza
Area Code 212 Tel. 264–0634

Philadelphia, Pennsylvania 19107
Jefferson Building
1015 Chestnut Street
Area Code 215 Tel. 597–2850

Phoenix, Arizona 85025
5413 New Federal Building
230 N. First Avenue
Area Code 602 Tel. 261–3285

Pittsburgh, Pennsylvania 15222
2201 Federal Building
1000 Liberty Avenue
Area Code 412 Tel. 644–2850

Portland, Oregon 97204
217 Old U.S. Courthouse
520 S.W. Morrison Street
Area Code 503 Tel. 226–3361

Reno, Nevada 89502
2028 Federal Building
300 Booth Street
Area Code 702 Tel. 784–5203

Richmond, Virginia 23240
2105 Federal Building
400 N. 8th Street
Area Code 703 Tel. 649–3611

St. Louis, Missouri 63103
2511 Federal Building
1520 Market Street
Area Code 314 Tel. 622–4243

Salt Lake City, Utah, 84111
3235 Federal Building
125 S. State Street
Area Code 801 Tel. 524–5116

San Francisco, California 94102
Federal Building
Box 36013
450 Golden Gate Avenue
Area Code 415 Tel. 556–5864

San Juan, Puerto Rico 00902
Room 100
Post Office Building
Phone 723–4640

Savannah, Georgia 31402
235 U.S. Courthouse and Post Office Building
125–29 Bull Street
Area Code 912 Tel. 232–4321

Seattle, Washington 98104
809 Federal Office Building
909 First Avenue
Area Code 206 Tel. 583–5615

Small Business Administration Offices Are Located in the Following Cities:

Agana, Guam
Alburquerque, New Mexico
Anchorage, Alaska
Atlanta, Georgia
Augusta, Maine
Baltimore, Maryland
Birmingham, Alabama
Boise, Idaho
Boston, Massachusetts
Buffalo, New York
Casper, Wyoming
Charleston, West Virginia
Charlotte, North Carolina
Chicago, Illinois
Cincinnati, Ohio
Clarksburg, West Virginia
Cleveland, Ohio
Columbia, South Carolina
Columbus, Ohio
Concord, New Hampshire
Dallas, Texas
Denver, Colorado
Des Moines, Iowa
Detroit, Michigan
Dover, Delaware
Fairbanks, Alaska
Fargo, North Dakota
Harlingen, Texas
Hartford, Connecticut
Hato Rey, Puerto Rico
Helena, Montana
Honolulu, Hawaii
Houston, Texas
Indianapolis, Ind.
Jackson, Mississippi
Jacksonville, Florida
Kansas City, Missouri
Knoxville, Tennessee
Las Vegas, Nevada

Little Rock, Arkansas
Los Angeles, California
Louisville, Kentucky
Lubbock, Texas
Madison, Wisconsin
Marquette, Michigan
Marshall, Texas
Miami, Florida
Milwaukee, Wisconsin
Minneapolis, Minnesota
Montpelier, Vermont
Nashville, Tennessee
Newark, New Jersey
New Orleans, Louisiana
New York, New York
Oklahoma City, Oklahoma
Omaha, Nebraska
Philadelphia, Pennsylvania
Phoenix, Arizona
Pittsburgh, Pennsylvania
Portland, Oregon
Providence, Rhode Island
Richmond, Virginia
St. Louis, Missouri
St. Thomas, Virgin Islands
Salt Lake City, Utah
San Antonio, Texas
San Diego, California
San Francisco, California
Seattle, Washington
Sioux Falls, South Dakota
Spokane, Washington
Syracuse, New York
Tampa, Florida
Toledo, Ohio
Tucson, Arizona
Washington, D. C.
Wichita, Kansas

For addresses and telephone numbers of the SBA Field Offices listed above, consult the appropriate telephone directory.

Both in Washington and in the regional offices you'll be almost embarrassed by the help the government consultant offers you. Often he will make a visit to your store, plant, or proposed location, to give you on-the-spot advice.

A thrifty tip: while much of the government printed material is free (and I stand by the title of this book absolutely!), a lot more is available at the cost of printing, which may range from a dime to several dollars. I've found, though, that if you pick up the books in the Field Offices of SBA, the Department of Commerce, or the other agencies we'll talk about later in this book, the man will usually hand them to you without charge. So, if it's not too much of a trip, drop in on the Field Office and use the Superintendent of Documents only when the Field Office is out of reach or out of stock.

WHAT BUSINESS FOR YOU? . . .

Thumb through the yellow pages of your telephone directory. There are a thousand businesses you could go into. Which shall it be? Let's assume you don't have your mind made up in advance; you aren't set on the flower business because you love flowers or on starting a health-food store because you believe in natural foods. You're open to suggestion. Good! Your Uncle Sam is Johnny on the spot with the best, the most complete, the most reliable information you can hope to get anywhere. He will flood you with printed material all aimed directly at your own problems.

For an over-all survey of the whole situation, we turn first to the Small Business Administration's wonderful Starting and Managing Series. These authoritative government books deal with key aspects of starting and managing a specific kind of small business. Here is a rundown on several books in this series.

1. *Starting and Managing a Small Business of Your Own.* Describes the common problems of launching small business operations in general, suggesting specific steps to help those interested in starting and managing a small business to arrive at sound decisions concerning these problems.

2. *Starting and Managing a Service Station.* Provides information of value to both the newcomer and the veteran service-station operator. For the prospective dealer, it provides a guide to operating conditions in the field—one that spells out for them both common problems and pitfalls as well as potential rewards. For those already in business, it discusses the broad area of administration and long-range planning.

3. *Starting and Managing a Small Bookkeeping Service.* This booklet should have a special appeal to prospective owner-managers of a small bookkeeping service. It discusses what public bookkeeping is like; what it also takes to start a small bookkeeping service; what services to provide; where to locate; what you will earn; what sort of organization you need; and planning for the future.

4. *Starting and Managing a Small Business of Your Own.* This volume is intended for prospective business owners. It answers questions such as: what business should you choose? How much money will you need? Where to get the money? What should you know about buying? What selling methods should you use?, and many more that may prove the key to success.

5. *Starting and Managing a Small Motel.* This publication, prepared to supply new and inexperienced owner-managers with basic management know-how, deals with the opportunities, risks, and problems involved in going into the motel business.

In addition to the above titles, you can also get the following books in this series:

Starting and Managing a Small Business of Your Own
Starting and Managing a Service Station
Starting and Managing a Small Bookkeeping Service
Starting and Managing a Small Building Business
Starting and Managing a Swap Shop or Consignment Sale Shop
Starting and Managing a Small Shoe Service Shop
Starting and Managing a Small Retail Camera Shop
Starting and Managing a Retail Flower Shop
Starting and Managing a Pet Shop
Starting and Managing a Small Retail Music Store
Starting and Managing a Small Retail Jewelry Store
Starting and Managing an Employment Agency
Starting and Managing a Small Drive-In Restaurant
Starting and Managing a Small Restaurant
Starting and Managing a Small Retail Hardware Store
Starting and Managing a Small Retail Drugstore
Starting and Managing a Small Drycleaning Business
Starting and Managing a Small Automatic Vending Business
Starting and Managing a Carwash

The titles in this list of the Starting and Managing Series range from 60 cents to $1.50 each. At random, let's look into one of these: *Starting and Managing a Small Building Business.*

For your 75 cents you get over 100 pages of solid know-how, condensed from a lifetime of experience by recognized experts in the field. Fourteen chapters take you through such problems as:

The final chapter directs you to sources for further information. This, incidentally, is standard with Government publications; they almost always wind up with a list of references to help you get still more knowledge about the subject under discussion.

I can personally cite a true example of how one of these books saved a friend of mine thousands of dollars. We were having lunch together one day, and he casually mentioned that he and his father were going to buy a motel the following day. I asked him what he knew about the motel business, and he replied, "Nothing at all, and neither does my father; but the place we're buying is a real gold mine! You should see the business they do each day!"

He went on to tell me that they had examined the owner's books, and he was ready to put his life savings and the life savings of his father into this new venture.

I persuaded him to go down to the offices of the Small Business Administration in Los Angeles and buy a copy of the book, *Starting and Managing a Small Motel*. He promised to buy the book and read it before he completed his negotiations on the purchase of the motel. Two days later he came into my office full of gratitude. He told me that this

40-cent book was responsible for saving him and his father their life savings. The book pointed out many facets of motel operation that he never suspected existed. It also told him what to look for when buying an established motel; and it was this particular information that opened his eyes to the poor investment he was ready to make.

But let's say that motels, service stations, or credit and collection are not your dish of tea. Will you have to wait until the SBA gets around to a booklet in this series on the business *you* are interested in? Not at all. SBA puts out forty-five Small Business Bibliographies. They cover a large number of businesses as well as some general problems common to all businesses. More of these bulletins are coming out all the time. They're absolutely free. Whether your taste runs to retailing, service industry, manufacturing, you'll find unbiased, factual, down-to-earth *expert* advice. The government has no ax to grind, no supplies to sell you, no fear of hurting your feelings with the hard truth where it will save you money, time, and grief.

Let's examine a couple of these bulletins to see the kind of information you're getting. Many of them are just bibliographies, a few pages long, telling you where to go for your information. Others are more complete. For instance, SBB No. 3, *Selling by Mail Order,* explains mail order rather fully, tells about the market, the kinds of goods to choose and the kinds to stay away from; it tells about proper pricing and markup and sources for getting your merchandise. You're told how to get or build a mailing list, how to key advertisements so you'll know which publications are pulling orders and which are wasting your advertising money. More data is given on rules and regulations you must know and follow: the postal rules, other federal laws; what to do about a firm name.

Then comes the list of government and other publications you can turn to for more information. This booklet, like all of the SBB series, costs you just a smile . . . no money!

Since mail order is my own business, I can vouch for the straight-from-the-shoulder, accurate information this SBB booklet contains. I have seen many commercial mail-order courses selling for as high as $100 that are far less illuminating than this free business booklet. If mail order is your cup of tea, another excellent Small Business Bulletin is No. 29, *National Mailing List Houses.* This is a directory of compilers or brokers of mailing lists of national scope. It tells you how to contact companies who deal in the business of renting names and addresses on different potential buyers for your products. To give you an idea of the diversity you'll find with the aid of this booklet, you can locate mailing lists of aviation manufacturing executives, elderly persons, farmers, fire chiefs, food brokers, hardware wholesalers, lawyers, mail-order buyers, ministers, newlyweds, opportunity seekers, single women, surgical-supply dealers, truck owners, veterans of the Korean conflict, wealthy persons, and wine distributors. How diversified can you get!

Two excellent SBB booklets are *Handcrafts and Home Businesses.* Both of these booklets can be quite valuable to a person wishing to go into business for himself. Handcrafts is directed to those people who have attained a degree of expertness in some craft or skill and would like to build a business based on it. Woodworking, textile arts, metal arts, small-animal raising, and cooking are among the many pursuits carried on around the home that sometimes become the nucleus for a successful business enterprise. While this publication does not provide complete coverage of handcrafts and home products made for profit, it points out the main considerations in a successful business of this sort and furnishes a few references to literature on a number of different crafts.

The booklet on *Home Businesses* is directed to those

people who have some spare time and are looking for a way to turn it to interesting and profitable use. The principal emphasis in this booklet is on the marketing of a product or service rather than on the creation of a product, and it deals primarily with those businesses that are essentially a one-man enterprise where the proprietor is working for profit and not a salary or a wage.

In addition to the booklets just described, there are at least sixty-five more SBB booklets now in print, with additional ones being added from time to time. Here's a list of SBB booklets now in print.

SMALL BUSINESS BIBLIOGRAPHIES
(No mailing list for this series)

These leaflets furnish reference sources for individual types of businesses.

1. *Handicrafts*
2. *Home Businesses*
3. *Selling by Mail Order*
9. *Marketing Research Procedures*
10. *Retailing*
12. *Statistics and Maps for National Market Analysis*
13. *National Directories for Use in Marketing*
14. *The Nursery Business*
15. *Recordkeeping Systems— Small Store and Service Trade*
17. *Restaurants and Catering*
18. *Basic Library Reference Sources*
20. *Advertising—Retail Store*
21. *Variety Stores*
24. *Food Stores*
27. *Suburban Shopping Centers*
29. *National Mailing-List Houses*
30. *Voluntary and Cooperative Food Chains*
31. *Retail Credit and Collections*
33. *Drugstores*
37. *Buying for Retail Stores*
41. *Mobile Homes and Parks*
42. *Bookstores*
44. *Job Printing Shop*
45. *Men's and Boys' Wear Stores*

46. *Woodworking Shops*
47. *Soft-Frozen Dessert Stands*
48. *Furniture Retailing*
50. *Apparel and Accessories for Women, Misses, & Children*
51. *Trucking and Cartage*
52. *Store Arrangement and Display*
53. *Hobby Shops*
55. *Wholesaling*
56. *Training Commercial Salesmen*
58. *Automation for Small Offices*
60. *Painting and Wall Decorating*
64. *Photographic Dealers and Studios*
65. *Real Estate Business*
66. *Motels*
67. *Manufacturers' Sales Representative*
68. *Discount Retailing*
69. *Machine Shop—Job Type*
72. *Personnel Management*
74. *Retail Florist*
75. *Inventory Management*
76. *Pet Shops*

One of the most informative books published by the Small Business Administration is entitled *A Survey of Federal Government Publications of Interest to Small Business* and its purpose is to provide, in a single volume, information about publications of interest to small business owners. From the vast output of booklets, pamphlets, and leaflets published by the various government agencies, those most likely to be of assistance to the small business sector are listed in this survey. Some are for sale at nominal prices by the Superintendent of Documents, and many others may be obtained at no cost from the issuing agencies. All are readily available to the small business owner-manager.

Some of the material listed in this survey outlines the help available from federal agencies. Other publications explain, in nontechnical language, the laws which the agencies enforce. Still others present statistical data useful in marketing or specialized information pertinent to particular industries or trades. Small business operators interested, for example, in obtaining a government contract, improving their management, or extending marketing operations abroad will find publications listed in this survey which will provide them with useful information. Prospective businessmen or students will also find helpful references on many subjects relating to small business management and operation.

To give you an idea of the scope of this book, here are a few of the many listings you'll find in it.

Costs of Operating Nursing Homes and Related Facilities
Advertising for Profit and Prestige
A Directory of Foreign Advertising Agencies and Marketing Research Organizations for the United States International Business Community
Sales Promotion Pointers for Small Retailers
Alaska: Its Economy and Market Potential
Selling to AEC (U.S. Atomic Energy Commission)
Special Sources of Information on Isotopes
USAEC Patents Available for Licensing
What's Available in the Atomic Energy Literature
Available Leaflets on Fisheries
Basic Library Reference Sources for Business Use
Catalog of United States Foreign Trade Statistical Publications
Data Sources for Plant Location Analysis
Federal Trade Commission List of Publications
List of Available Publications of the United States Department of Agriculture
Mobile Homes
Selected List of Publications on Social Security
Small Business Administration Publications
Small Plant Turnover and Failure
General Information on Copyright
Directory of National Associations of Businessmen
Direct Methods of Selling in Foreign Markets
Facts About Small Business Financing
Helping the Banker Help You

The Market for Food in Public Schools
Restaurants and Other Eating Places
Retail Produce Manual
Selling to Navy Prime Contractors
Selling Business Pooling for Defense, Production, Research and Development
Small Business Specialists and Advisers by Organization and States

BUTCHER, BAKER, CANDLESTICK MAKER?

Already it's clear that you'd better not plunge into some business for yourself without hard thinking, planning, even soul searching. Even if you've had experience in some other business or as an employee of a firm, large or small, you might not be aware of a vital detail which could mean success or failure.

More than 1,000 new businesses are started in the United States each day, including more than 900 businesses transferred from one owner to another. But get this: 930 businesses are *discontinued* each day! Such a turnover in business ownership indicates a real need for information about the responsibilities of starting and managing a business.

When you consider that you have at your disposal, through the Small Business Administration, the talents and brains of some of the best business heads in the country, it is really a crime to start any business endeavor without first taking advantage of the advice and help available to you. You're paying for these services with your taxes. Take advantage of them!

WHAT ABOUT THE MONEY? . . .

All right. You've decided you're the type to succeed. You have some idea of what business you want to engage in. Next question: Capital.

Uncle Sam is right there to help you. Next to the veteran, the home buyer, and the farmer, he loves the small businessman the best.

We've listed here a number of agencies set up primarily to help finance either a starting or a going business.

1. Small Business Investment Companies (SBIC)

Small business investment companies may make long-term loans to incorporated and unincorporated small businesses in order to provide funds needed for sound financing, growth, modernization and expansion. Long-term loans, as used herein, mean loans with final maturities of not less than 5 years and not more than 20 years.

An SBIC's long-term loan must be of such sound value, or so secured, as reasonably to assure repayment. They may bear interest at rates agreed upon between the SBIC and the borrower. However, the rate of interest may not exceed the maximum rate permitted by local law; where no local limit is fixed, the interest rate charged must be within the rate limits set forth in the SBIC's proposal for a license.

2. G.I. Business Loans

If you're a veteran and haven't used up your whole "entitlement," the Veterans Administration may guarantee part of a loan you need to undertake or expand a legitimate business or even to pay off delinquent debts incurred in your venture.

3. Federal Reserve Bank Loans

Again, you must first apply to a bank, as these loans are available only if loans through private sources cannot be obtained on reasonable terms. The Federal Reserve Banks are located in Boston, New York City, Philadelphia, Cleveland, Richmond, Atlanta, Chicago, St. Louis, Minneapolis, Kansas City, Dallas, and San Francisco. And there are branches in twenty-four other cities.

4. Export-Import Bank of Washington

This agency aids in financing to facilitate foreign trade. Again, first apply through your local bank.

5. Miscellany

Loans for farmers are handled through the Department of Agriculture, and loans for veterans through the Veterans Administration.

6. The Small Business Administration

The SBA itself maintains offices of Loan Administration and Processing to lend money to start and carry on small business ventures. We'll talk more about this in the chapters to come.

Then there is money available under the Area Redevelopment Act to help you locate or expand in an area where employment is down. See Chapter III for more on this.

The congressional Declaration of Policy in the Small Business Act states: "The Government should aid, counsel, assist, and protect, insofar as is possible, the interests of small business concerns in order to preserve free competitive enterprise . . . and to maintain and strengthen the overall economy of the Nation."

With all the assistance the government is ready to give, you will have to admit that they are living up to their "Declaration of Policy."

BIBLIOGRAPHY

Department of Commerce Publications (annual)
  1972 Supplement 75¢ (available Government Printing
  Office and Commerce Dept. Field Offices)
Small Business Administration (Starting and Managing
  Series):
  A Small Business of Your Own $1.05
  A Service Station 70 cents
  A Small Bookkeeping Service 75 cents
  A Small Building Business 75 cents
  A Small Restaurant $1.20 cents
  A Small Retail Hardware Store 90 cents
  A Small Retail Drugstore $1.25
  A Small Dry Cleaning Business 70 cents
  A Small Automatic Vending Business 75 cents
  A Small Carwash 90 cents
  A Swap Shop or Consignment Sale Shop 95 cents
  A Small Service Shoe Shop $1.00
  A Small Retail Camera Shop 80 cents
  A Retail Flower Shop $1.20
  A Pet Shop 60 cents
  A Small Retail Music Store $1.30
  A Small Retail Jewelry Store 90 cents
  An Employment Agency $1.30
  A Small Drive-In Restaurant 75 cents
A Survey of Federal Government Publications of Interest
  to Small Business:
Note: To get these and all other publications we'll be
      mentioning in chapters to come
  (a) Go to the regional branch office of the department
      or agency which issues the publication; or
  (b) write to the main headquarters of the Dept. or
      agency; or
  (c) write to the Superintendent of Documents Wash-
      ington, D. C. 20402; or
  (d) go to any of the 480-plus Depository Libraries to
      read the material (Addresses of the libraries are

listed in the U. S. Department of Commerce Publications, 1972 Supplement 75¢)

(e) go to the nearest Government Printing Office Bookstores listed below:

Government Printing Office
710 North Capitol Street
Washington, D.C. 20402
Telephone: Area code 202–783-3238

Forrestal Bookstore
Room 1-J-001
James Forrestal Building
1000 Independence Ave.
(L'Enfant Plaza)
Washington, D.C. 20407
Telephone: Area code 202–426-7937

Department of Commerce, Lobby
14th and Constitution Avenue NW.
Washington, D.C. 20230
Telephone: Area code 202–967-3527

Atlanta Bookstore
Room 100, Federal Building
275 Peachtree Street NE.
Atlanta, Georgia 30303
Telephone: Area code 404–526-6947

Birmingham Bookstore
Room 102A, 2121 Building
2121 Eighth Avenue North
Birmingham, Alabama 35203
Telephone: Area code 205–325-6056

Boston Bookstore
Room G25, John F. Kennedy Federal Building
Sudbury Street
Boston, Massachusetts 02203
Telephone: Area code 617–223-6071

Canton, Ohio Bookstore
Federal Office Building
201 Cleveland Avenue SW.
Canton, Ohio 44702
Telephone: Area code 216–455-8971

Chicago Bookstore
Room 1463–14th floor
Everett McKinley Dirksen Building
219 South Dearborn Street
Chicago, Illinois 60604
Telephone: Area code 312–353-5133

Dallas Bookstore
Room 1C46
Federal Building–U.S. Courthouse
1100 Commerce Street
Dallas, Texas 75202
Telephone: Area code 214–749-1541

Detroit Bookstore
Room 229, Federal Building
231 W. Lafayette Blvd.
Detroit, Michigan 48226
Telephone: Area code 313–226-7816

Denver Bookstore
Room 1421
Federal Building–U.S. Courthouse
1961 Stout Street
Denver, Colorado 80202
Telephone: Area code 303–837-3965

Kansas City Bookstore
Room 135, Federal Office Building
601 East 12th Street
Kansas City, Missouri 64106
Telephone: Area code 816–374-2160

Los Angeles Bookstore
Room 1015, Federal Office Building
300 North Los Angeles Street
Los Angeles, California 90012
Telephone: Area code 213–688-5841

New York Bookstore
Room 110
26 Federal Plaza
New York, New York 10007
Telephone: Area code 212–264-3826

Philadelphia Bookstore
U.S. Post Office and Courthouse
Main Lobby
Ninth and Chestnut Streets
Philadelphia, Pennsylvania 19107
Telephone: Area code 215–597-0677

San Francisco Bookstore
Room 1023, Federal Office Building

450 Golden Gate Avenue
San Francisco, California 94102
Telephone: Area code 415–556-6657

Cleveland Bookstore
1st Floor, Federal Office Bldg.
1240 East 9th Street
Cleveland, Ohio 44114

Seattle Bookstore
Room 194, Federal Office Bldg.
915 First Ave.
Seattle, Wash. 98104

Milwaukee Bookstore
Room 190, Federal Bldg.
519 Wisconsin Avenue
Milwaukee, Wisconsin 53202

Jacksonville Bookstore
Room 158 Federal Bldg.
400 West Bay Street
Jacksonville, Florida 32202

CHAPTER II

UNCLE SAM AS YOUR BUSINESS ADVISER

Running Your Own Business with Government Help

UNCLE SAM IS "JOHNNY ON THE SPOT" . . .

Almost everyone in this country remembers the terrible disaster which took place in my city some time ago: the bursting of the Baldwin Hills dam in Los Angeles. Within twenty-four hours after that nightmare event, before the victims even had a chance to come out of their shock and give a thought to the crushing blow they had sustained in the destruction of several millions of dollars in property, the Small Business Administration had set up makeshift offices in nearby schools and was offering long-term 3 per cent government loans to businessmen whose shops and stores had been gutted and whose fixtures and stocks were destroyed by water, mud, and contamination.

This is a dramatic example of Uncle Sam's going beyond the call of duty to keep the businessman on an even keel, no matter what problems he may run into. Let's hope that *your* business is never hit by a flood or other disaster. Even without such extremes, you'll have problems enough. But Uncle is right there to help out with your little headaches as well as your big ones.

All right, enough of morbid thoughts. You're established in business; you've got your retail, wholesale, service, or manufacturing organization going. What can you expect from your beneficent Uncle Sam?

The answer is . . . plenty!

We've been talking about loans, money. The sources of loans listed in Chapter I are not earmarked for *starting* businesses alone. You're perfectly welcome to tap these agencies for money to get over the difficult first years, or to wait out a bad season, or to carry you through a period of poor-paying customers, or to help a business "even out" the rough spots, wherever they occur. If you have a business you believe in, in which you've invested your own time, sweat, and money, many times it's worth the added risk of borrowing to keep it going. So keep those agencies alive in the back of your mind. Maybe you won't need them, but it's mighty comforting to know that they're around if you do.

THE DEPARTMENT OF COMMERCE . . .

In the previous chapter we told you something of the help offered by the Department of Commerce for beginners in business. By its very nature, this department is geared to help business in every stage, and practically all the material we'll discuss in this chapter originates there. At the risk of repeating a few things, I believe it's worth pounding away at the work of this great agency.

In general, from Honolulu to Boston, from Miami to Seattle, the Field Offices of the United States Department of Commerce are "in business to aid business." Every business firm and organization is a welcome "client" at the Commerce Field Office in its locality. The basic job of each Field Office is to help make business better in its area and to aid local business firms in improving and expanding their operations. The Field Office brings the resources and services of the Commerce Department to your doorstep.

A Local Department of Commerce

In effect, each Field Office is a small-scale Department of Commerce in its own locality. The offices are usually located in business centers so that services of the U. S. Department of Commerce will be more immediately available to businessmen. Accordingly, letters to the Department in Washington are often referred to a Field Office, and a businessman who needs prompt service usually finds it advisable to consult his Field Office directly. The Field Office also gives out Census Bureau data and serves as a local information center for other Commerce agencies, including the National Bureau of Standards, U.S. Patent Office, U.S. Travel Service, and Area Redevelopment Administration. In addition, the Field Office advises and assists you in matters pertaining to the Agency for International Development (AID).

Bank, and the Foreign Credit Insurance Corporation (FCIC).

A Trained Staff of Business Specialists

At each Field Office, experienced business specialists will assist you in the solution of business problems, furnish information and publications on the programs and services of the Commerce Department and other federal agencies, and provide counsel on both foreign and domestic business operations. These trained staff members are also available to address business groups in the area.

A Wide Range of Business Publications

Each Field Office maintains an extensive business library of government and private reports, publications, periodicals, and directories. It also stocks and sells many useful publications on business subjects issued by the Superintendent of Documents for your convenience.

Domestic Trade

The Field Offices have a vital part in carrying out the Commerce Department's statutory responsibility to "foster, promote and develop the foreign and domestic commerce . . . of the United States."

To encourage and assist your domestic trade, each Field Office can furnish current, accurate, and dependable information on:

American Business and Industry—including material on production, output, sales, raw material sources, industry trends and prospects, marketing practices, location factors, and the operation of wholesale, retail, and service businesses.

American Science and Technology—including information on new discoveries and inventions, new products and processes, patent licensing, industrial standards, and the utilization of new technical knowledge and methods.

The American People—including facts on population, migration trends, housing, personal income, consumer markets, buying patterns, and employment.

The American Economy—including material on national income, the national product, national and regional economic trends, domestic markets and market potentials, balance of payments, foreign-aid programs, and business indexes, indicators, and forecasts.

Each Field Office Director and his staff of business specialists is anxious to help increase your domestic business activity in his area and to help local businesses expand and prosper.

At each Field Office, the facilities and services of the Commerce Department are free to all types of business firms, trade and professional associations, advertising agencies, communications media, local and state government agencies, and other persons and organizations interested in business matters.

Co-operative Offices in More than 500 Locations

To make the Commerce Department's facilities and services even more accessible to you, some 560 business organizations located in fifty states and Puerto Rico are serving their areas as "Co-operative Offices" of the United States Department of Commerce. Be sure to ask your Field Office where the nearest "Co-op" in your line is located.

These organizations include local and state Chambers of Commerce, manufacturers' associations, and state and municipal development commissions. Each maintains close liaison with the Field Office serving its area.

In these Co-operative Offices, many of the department's reports and publications are available for reference use. Business problems requiring counsel and assistance not available at a Co-operative Office will be referred to the nearest Field Office of the department.

AND THAT AIN'T ALL!

All this tells only a part of what the Department does for the businessman. In a later chapter, for example, we'll take up the astounding variety of services it offers the businessman who wants to expand into foreign trade through the department's Bureau of International Commerce.

But for the purposes of this chapter, we'll confine ourselves to another bureau we've already mentioned: the Small Business Administration.

Go back and look again at the list of *Small Business*

Bulletins. In the last chapter we discussed them in terms of starting your business. Now that you glance over the list again, you'll see that a great many of them are slanted just as much toward helping you *run* your business, once it's under way. For example, take SBB (Small Business Bibliography) No. 9, *Market Research Procedures.* Furthermore, throughout the series, tips and information useful in operating a going business are scattered like plums in a pudding. And, of course, the references—the books and publications which you're led to examine through the suggestions in the bulletins—will contain still more information on keeping your business head above water, once you've plunged into the drink!

However, all this is just the appetizer before the feast. The Small Business Administration publishes still more books or booklets which come right to the "meat and potatoes" for the operating businessman. The booklets are broken down into four major categories:

1. Management Aids
2. Technical Aids
3. Small Marketers Aids
4. Small Business Bibliographies

Altogether they add up to more than 150 titles, and all are free.

Here are some of the more important of the titles in these four categories of booklets. Check off the numbers you're interested in.

FREE MANAGEMENT ASSISTANCE PUBLICATIONS

Management Aids

These leaflets deal with functional problems in small manufacturing plants and concentrate on subjects of interest to administrative executives.

Technical Aids

These leaflets are intended for top technical personnel in small concerns or for technical specialists who supervise that part of the company's operations.

Small Marketers Aids

These leaflets provide suggestions and management guidelines for small retail, wholesale, and service firms.

LIKE BANANAS, THEY COME IN BUNCHES . . .

In addition to the Technical Aids, Small Marketers Aids and Management Aids which are free from the Small Business Administration, the SBA puts out a Management Development Series. These may be ordered from the Superintendent of Documents as follows:

Management Development Series

Topic 2 *Records and Credit in Profitable Management*
Topic 5 *Financing—Short and Long Term Needs*
Topic 7 *Aspects of Sales Promotion*
Topic 9 *Communication and Control*
Topic 11 *Choosing a Form of Business Organization*
Topic 13 *Small Business Location and Layout*
Topic 14 *Effective Advertising*
Topic 15 *Sources of Assistance and Information*
Topic 16 *Why Customers Buy (and Why They Don't)*
Topic 20 *Merchandise Pricing*
Topic 21 *Merchandise Control*

The Small Business Management Series contains fuller, more detailed studies of management problems costing from 60 cents to $2.50. Here are thirty current titles (and don't forget that new ones are being added all the time.)

Small Business Management Series

The booklets in this series provide discussions of special management problems in small companies.

An Employee Suggestion System for Small Companies. SBA 1.12:1 18 pp. 40 cents. Explains the basic principles for starting and operating a suggestion system. It also warns of various pitfalls and gives examples of suggestions submitted by employees through company suggestion systems.

Human Relations in Small Business. SBA 1.12:3 68 pp. 60 cents. Discusses human relations as the subject involves finding and selecting employees, developing them, and motivating them.

Improving Material Handling in Small Business. SBA 1.12:4 42 pp. 70 cents. A discussion of the basics of the material handling function, the method of laying out workplaces, and other factors to setting up an efficient system.

Better Communications in Small Business. SBA 1.12:7 37 pp. 65 cents. Designed to help smaller manufacturers help themselves in winning cooperation by means of more skillful communications. It also seeks to explain how the controlling of communications within the firm can improve operating efficiency and competitive strength.

Cost Accounting for Small Manufacturers. SBA 1.12:9 163 pp. $1.60. Stresses the importance of determining and recording costs accurately. Designed for small manufacturers and their accountants. Diagrams, flow charts, and illustrations are included to make the material easier to use.

The Small Manufacturer and His Specialized Staff. SBA 1.12:13 36 pp. 65 cents. Stresses the necessity of building a competent staff through the use of staff specialist and outside professional advisers so that the small businessman can be relieved of routine work as the business prospers.

Handbook of Small Business Finance. SBA 1.12:15 80 pp. 95 cents. Written for the small businessman who wants to improve his financial-management skills. Indicates the major areas of financial management and describes a few of the many techniques that can help the small businessman understand and apply results of his past decisions to those of the future.

Franchise Index/Profile. SBA 1.12:35 56 pp. 65 cents. Presents an evaluation process that may be used to investigate franchise opportunities. The Index tells what to look for in a franchise. The Profile is a worksheet for listing the data.

Health Maintenance Programs for Small Business. SBA 1.12:16 64 pp. 70 cents. Discusses how smaller firms with limited fund can set up health programs to keep losses due to employee sickness and accidents as low as possible.

New Product Introduction for Small Business Owners. SBA 1.12:17 69 pp. 90 cents. Provides basic information which will help the owners of small businesses to understand better what is involved in placing a new or improved product on the market.

Technology and Your New Products. SBA 1.12:19 61 pp. 75 cents. Designed to inform the small businessman about the benefits of technology. For example, he can use technology to improve a product, to diversify a product line, and to reduce costs.

Ratio Analysis for Small Business. SBA 1.12:20 65 pp. 70 cents. Ratio analysis is the process of determining the relationships between certain financial or operating data of a business to provide a basis for managerial control. The purpose of the booklet is to help the owner-manager in detecting favorable or unfavorable trends in his business.

Profitable Small Plant Layout. SBA 1.12:21 48 pp. 65 cents. Help for the small business owner who is in the predicament of rising costs on finished goods, decreasing net profits, and lowered production because of the lack of economical and orderly movement of production materials from one process to another throughout the shop.

Guides for Profit Planning. SBA 1.12:25 52 pp. 70 cents. Guides for computing and using the breakeven point, the level of gross profit, and the rate of return on investment. Designed for readers who have no specialized training in accounting and economics.

Profitable Community Relations for Small Business. SBA 1.12:27 36 pp. 55 cents. Practical information on how to build and maintain sound community relations by participation in community affairs.

Management Audit for Small Manufacturers. SBA 1. 12:29 58 pp. 65 cents. A series of questions which will indicate whether the owner-manager of a small manufacturing plant is planning, organizing, directing, and coordinating his business activities efficiently.

Insurance and Risk Management for Small Business. SBA 1.12:30 72 pp. 80 cents. A discussion of what insurance is, the necessity of obtaining professional advice on buying insurance, and the main types of insurance a small business may need.

Management Audit for Small Retailers. SBA 1.12:31 50 pp. 65 cents. Designed to meet the needs of the owner-manager of a small retail enterprise. The approach is the same as that in SBMS No. 29—a do-it-yourself technique. That is, 149 questions guide the owner-manager in an examination of himself and his business operation.

Financial Recordkeeping for Small Stores. SBA 1.12:32 131 pp. $1.30. Written primarily for the small store owner or prospective owner whose business doesn't justify hiring a trained, full-time bookkeeper.

Small Store Planning for Growth. SBA 1.12:33 99 pp. $1.35. A discussion of the nature of growth, the management skills needed, and some techniques for use in promoting growth. Included is a consideration of merchandising, advertising and display, and checklists for increases in transactions and gross margins.

Selecting Advertising Media—A Guide for Small Business. SBA 1.12:34 120 pp. $1.40. Intended to aid the small businessman in deciding which medium to select for making his product, service, or store known to potential customers and how to make the most use of his advertising money.

Export Marketing for Smaller Firms. SBA 1.19:EX7/971 134 pp. $1.30.

Cash Planning in Small Manufacturing Companies. SBA 1.20:1 276 pp. $2.25. This book reports on research that was done on cash planning for the small manufacturer. It is designed for owners and managers of small firms and the specialists who study and aid small businesses.

The First Two Years: Problems of Small Firm Growth and Survival. SBA 1.20:2 23 pp. $2.40. This discussion is based on the detailed observation of 81 small retail and service firms over a 2-year period. The operations of each enterprise were systematically followed from the time of launching through the end of the second year.

Interbusiness Financing: The Economic Implications for Small Business. SBA 1.20:3 157 pp. $1.50. Interbusiness financing can be generally defined as the financial help that one independent business gives another without going through conventional sources such as banks and finance companies. This booklet tries to bring into focus the various methods used for this particular kind of assistance.

Personality and Success: An Evaluation of Personal Characteristics of Successful Small Business Managers. SBA 1.20:4 84 pp. $1.05. One of the major goals of the study reported in this book was to determine those personality traits of a successful business manager which contributed measurably to the success of his enterprise.

U.S. Government Purchasing and Sales Directory. SBA

1.13/3:972 169 pp. $2.35. A directory for businesses
that are interested in selling to the U.S. Government.
Lists the purchasing needs of various Agencies.

Managing for Profits. SBA 1.2:M31/11 170 pp. $1.60. Ten
chapters on various aspects of small business management, for example: marketing, production, and credit.

Buying and Selling a Small Business. SBA 1.2:B98 122 pp.
$1.25. Deals with the problems that confront buyers
and sellers of small businesses. Discusses the buy-sell
transaction, sources of information for buyer-seller decision, the buy-sell process, using financial statements in
the buy-sell transaction, and analyzing the market position of the company.

Strengthening Small Business Management. SBA
1.2:M31/14 158 pp. $1.85. Twenty-one chapters on
small business management. This collection reflects the
experience which the author gained in a life time of
work with the small business community.

These Small Business Management Series are not bibliographies or pamphlets, but books of 50 to 100 or more pages,
covering all aspects and sides of the subject. Let's take a
closer look at one of them.

Small Business Management Series No. 24, *Selecting
Advertising Media—A Guide for Small Business.* Suppose
you're a small manufacturer of industrial goods—fabricated
metal products for construction, let's say. Should you advertise? How much should you budget for advertising? How
should you choose an agency? What will be the functions of
your own advertising manager? Does advertising pay in a
product like yours, anyway?

These and a thousand other questions you'd be asking
yourself about advertising are answered here. Note first how
the booklet doesn't attempt to cover *all* advertising situations. Even in the manufacturing field, it limits its range to

industrial products. Advertising for consumers' products is covered in other places.

Thus advertising is put in its proper place: along with your salesmen, as a sales tool you can't afford to do without any more than you'd cut out your sales staff.

The booklet goes on to help you set your advertising objectives and then proceeds to the organization problems: planning, and selecting your advertising manager and advertising agency.

I'd say that 99 out of 100 small businessmen wouldn't know the first thing about how to select an agency. It's as risky as selecting a wife; but, fortunately, a few rules can be laid down about picking an agency! The book's very first word on the subject can save you endless grief: "Never select an agency for purely personal reasons. The fact that it's run by your brother-in-law doesn't make it the right agency for you. Matter of fact, that very relationship can make it the *wrong* one."

But you can check into the prospective agency's qualifications by asking what success they've had with other clients, digging into their reputation (even among competitors), examining the training and experience of the people in the agency, getting a line on their creative abilities and imagination and what they know about markets, media, etc. How long have the present clients been with the agency? How many have they lost over the last few years?

After a grilling like this, you'll have a pretty good idea of what you're getting into. But the book doesn't stop with putting you into the agency's hands. It continues, educating you on sound advertising practices, covering newspaper, periodical, direct-mail, and other types; it tells you how to evaluate results, how to keep records, and gives many other pointers. It concludes with actual case histories and the usual list of solid books, magazines, and other places to get still more information. This could be the best thirty-five-cent investment you've ever made!

HOW TO READ AN ACCOUNT BOOK . . .

When Abe Lincoln ran his log-cabin general store, he figured that if he bought a cord of wood from a farmer for a dollar and sold it to a householder for two dollars, he made a dollar profit. Business *used* to be that simple, but no longer. Abe didn't have to pay rent for his store or the land it stood on, didn't advertise or count interest on his invested capital, didn't have a payroll, didn't figure in the value of his own time or the depreciation on his tools. His selling price on the wood—his "ratio" of sales to cost—was two to one.

Today, if you try to work on Abe's figures, you'll probably be operating at a *loss* because cost is only one of the many factors (some hidden) you have to take into account in setting your selling price to come out ahead. That's why, before leaving this absolutely diamond-studded series of *Small Business Management* pamphlets, I want to give you a bird's-eye view of just one more. This is No. 20, *Ratio Analysis for Small Business.* Ratio is not the easiest thing in the world to grasp, but it can mean the difference between business failure and success because, the author points out, most small-business failures are due to weaknesses in the *management* of the business. In spite of the advantages of small business—simplicity, adaptability, quick decision possibilities, and the like —the small-business manager has to wear many hats. Some fit him better than others.

Do you know how to figure in every expense and overhead item in setting *your* selling costs? What are your policies on credit—especially the borderline risk cases? How's your inventory control in relation to your sales and operating capital? Are you counting in assets like real estate, machinery, equipment, and fixtures when figuring your capital? How do you manage your current and long term liabilities? Are you keeping future growth in mind and setting aside money to finance it?

If any of these questions cause you to scratch *your* head, this is a book for you to read. I don't go into the technical details; that's something for you to work out with your accountant. But a case history cited in the book may give you a graphic idea of some possible shortcomings of your own. I'll just quote part of it.

The banker motioned to his visitor. "Come in, Dave; sit down." When Dave was seated, Tompkins opened his desk drawer and pulled out a group of sheets containing columns of figures posted on comparative forms. The lumberman guessed that they were his.

"Glad you came in. I've been wanting to have a chat with you for quite a while." Then followed a moment of silence as the banker stared out the window. Finally, he continued: "Dave, you're a good salesman, and you know lumber. How well do you know your own figures?"

"I don't know, Mr. Tompkins. The bookkeeper gives me monthly statements—sales, cash, and expenses. She runs off a balance sheet once a year when we take inventory—taxes, you know, and all that. Most of the time, I'm too busy in the yard to go into the ledgers. I leave most of the details to her."

The banker waited and then went on. "Let me ask you another question, Dave. Why do you insist on doing business for nothing?" Dave was startled, and he began to flush. He had been expecting to be taken to task for the overdue note, and had thought himself reasonably well fortified with reasons. But the conversation was now taking a turn for which he was unprepared.

"I'm *not* working for nothing," Dave countered. "Last two years, it's been tough. I've been building up business—you know that. Look at my history. I'm worth more than . . ."

"Wait a minute, Dave. I know what you're going to say. But just look at your figures. Last year, you netted $1,700. The year before, it was $750, and that was before your taxes. You could have done better working for someone else. Lots of yards would have been glad to have you as a salesman or yard manager at your same salary and profit. You made virtually nothing on invested capital."

"But how much should I have made?" Dave asked.

"You know, Dave, the amount of profit a concern 'should earn' on its capital is something of an academic question. Some say that the ratio of net profits after taxes to tangible net worth should be between 5 and 10 percent. I look at it this way: If you'd gone to work for someone else, and invested your $64,000 in blue chip securities, you could have safely earned around 5 per cent in dividends. That's—let's see, nearly $3,100—almost twice your earnings before taxes.

"Anyway, let's be practical. Your net profit on net sales for the year was just under one-half of 1 per cent. Your State Association of Lumber Dealers reports that its studies indicate an average return for its members of close to 3½ per cent on sales—7 times what you're getting."

Dave was quiet. The point had been driven home. The banker softened. "Of course, Dave, when you missed receiving your 2 per cent discount on some $300,000 in purchases, I know that it hurt."

"Sure," Dave came back, "but it takes money to take discounts. Why if I had more capital—say $40,000 more —it would be a cinch. But where would I lay my hands on that kind of cash?"

"Maybe, Dave, you've got all the capital you're going to need," said the banker, as he spread out the Middleville

Lumber Co.'s figures over his desk. "You know, Dave, I'm convinced you have been violating three commandments of financial management."

"Now, wait a moment, Mr. Tompkins!" Dave countered. "You know as well as I do, I'll never borrow a dime I can't pay back, nor buy a two-by-four I won't pay for. I'm solvent. Look at my figures. I've got assets to pay."

As Dave broke off, the banker picked up the figures and continued, "Don't get upset. I know you're honest, and I know your intentions. If we weren't sure about that, I wouldn't be talking to you. I'm thinking of something else. The three commandments I mentioned are something I heard a speaker refer to once. They are: Don't overbuy, don't overtrade, don't overexpand. Now don't you agree you've done all three?"

Dave hedged, "Well—what makes you think so?"

"Look here." The banker and the lumberman drew up their chairs. "Let's start with your balance sheet. You show current assets of $130,000 and current debts of $88,000. Your current ratio is 1.47 to 1. That's dangerously close according to your association. They've felt that the average lumberyard should show—at a minimum—a ratio of 3 to 1. Other studies I've seen indicate a prevailing median current ratio of 3.4 to 1. So to my eye you look low on current ratio.

"Now take your working capital—current assets less current debts. In your case, it's $42,000. That's the money you would have left over, if you were to suddenly pay off all debts by liquidating current assets. It's the protective cushion you need to have in carrying your receivables and inventory. Last year, your ratio of working capital to net sales was about nine times. Experience suggests to me that four times would have been about right. Take your turnover of tangible net worth; by that I mean the ratio of your $66,000 in tangible net worth to $363,000 in net sales. It was nearly five and one-half times for the year. My observation is that it should have been a little more than two and one-half times. I'm basing that comment on some 'standard' ratios I obtained for the comparison. That's why I say I think you've been overtrading."

"What does all this standard-ratio stuff mean?" Dave interjected. "That fast figure work was a little over my head."

"It's simple enough if you figure it out in logical order, Dave. Overtrading with finances is something like speeding in a car. At 30 miles an hour, a blowout is an inconvenience—but at 80 miles an hour?"

Tompkins paused to let the point sink in.

"Look, Dave—what if one of your big customers goes sour and you have to write some big receivables off as bad debts? What if prices take a quick tumble and your inventory declines in value? What if building should suddenly come to a halt in this area because of a strike? How about your own health—what if you were to be sick? Suppose creditors demand their own money?

"Suppose . . ." and the banker smiled, "Suppose, Dave, we called your loan."

Dave glanced up quickly. "Okay, Mr. Tompkins, I see the point. How about the loan?"

"Let's think some things through first, Dave. We'll get to the loan—and we don't intend to see you forced out of business. But let's understand this: a soundly operated business has the strength to sustain blowouts. You haven't."

And that's about all we need of that, I guess. For the rest of the story, read the book. But maybe the little sample I quoted will make you re-examine your own buying, borrowing, pricing policies. Are they based on sound principles? Or do you just throw darts at a board to pick out the figures? If you're a "Dave," you'd better straighten up and fly right. As the friendly banker concluded, Dave was a good businessman, all right; he was just shy on certain knowledge he needed to make his business solid, sound, and profitable.

The book you're holding in your hand tells you how to get $100,000 worth of business advice from the United States Government.

Well, maybe in the past couple of pages you've already had your $100,000 worth. If so, the following chapters are pure gravy for you!

BIBLIOGRAPHY

Small Business Administration.

Selecting Advertising Media—A Guide for Small Business (Small Business Management Series No. 24) $1.40

Ratio Analysis for Small Businesses (Small Business Management Series No. 20) 70 cents

Effective Advertising (Management Development Series— Topic 14)

A Survey of Federal Government publications of Interest to Small Business

CHAPTER III

UNCLE SAM AS YOUR
SALES PROMOTION MAN

BUILDING YOUR BUSINESS
WITH GOVERNMENT HELP

Once you've decided on your business, once you've got it rolling on an even keel, you can't just sit back and relax. Far from it! You've got to grab that car and keep moving forward.

Or, to put it in another way, you must recognize the unwritten rule of business, particularly American business: Progress or die.

And unless you keep constantly on the lookout for new ideas, new sources, fresh products to fit into your line, new uses for old products, and new markets for products both old and new, you can take it from me . . . your business will strangle and die.

Uncle Sam has been anxious to set you up in business and to point you in the right direction. He's just as anxious to give you a push when you falter. In this chapter, let's look into the aids for increasing your profits against the many elements which are constantly chipping away at them. In other words, let's see what your government can do to help you stay afloat in today's highly competitive market.

SOME BASICS . . .

There was a time when you could mind your own store and let the world take care of itself. Those days are gone. Today's businessman cannot remain content with a knowledge merely of his own line, his own industry and market area.

Recognizing this, the government supplies you with information about national and international conditions and changes affecting all business in general, plus your own business in particular. These changing conditions are kept up to the minute through a listing of the Department of Commerce: Bureau of Census Catalog.

This is one of your sources for getting hold of the information you need to help you run your business and increase profits. Naturally, a good deal of the material will not pertain to your specific enterprise, but it's unlikely that you could thumb through an issue and not come upon something you can use. And remember, one little idea can be worth thousands of dollars.

Let's examine a typical copy of this basic information source. It opens with Census and General Business Statistics, offering about a dozen entries, already published or to be published shortly, in the areas of agriculture, business, governments, housing, manufactures, minerals, population.

Other sections cover domestic trade, foreign trade, etc., and tell you about the latest publications in these fields, what they cost, and where you can get them.

A sampling of a few of these entries gives some idea of the value you can expect from this periodical.

Annual Survey of Manufactures C56.221/2/970–71 Annual (prices vary). Number of manufacturing plants classified by industry, state, county and employment-size class.

1963 Census of Manufactures of Puerto Rico; MC63-

PR, Puerto Rico. Data on manufacturing establishments in Puerto Rico are presented in five chapters: General Statistics, Industry Statistics, Area Statistics, Tax-exempt Establishments and Local and Nonlocal Ownership Covering Puerto Rico, regions, subregions, planning areas, SMSA's, municipios.

Statistical Abstract of the United States. Annual. CS 1.34:974 $10.20 cloth, $6.85 paper. The one-volume basic reference source is standard summary of statistics on social, political, and economic organization of the United States. Includes comprehensive selection of data from most important statistical publications, both governmental and private, and an extensive bibliography of statistical sources. Contains over 1,200 tables and charts.

Canned Food Report. Series B1. Issued five times a year. Subscription, $1.00 per season, single copy 25 cents. Bureau of the Census. Data on stocks of wholesale distributors, canners, and warehouses of retail food chains. Coverage is for canned food items (vegetables, fruits, juices, and fish).

Travel During 1972, C56.246/2:TC 72-N3 $2.45. Bureau of the Census. Presents data on overnight trips or one-day trips to a place at least 100 miles (one way) from traveler's home. Detail tables on number of trips and trip days in business travel, personal trips to visit friends and relatives, vacation trips, and other travel. Shows means of transportation, distance to major destinations, income level of traveler, and other factors.

Catalog of Federal Domestic Assistance Pr. Ex. $2.20 Subscription $14.50.

General Information Concerning Patents. 39 pp., 45 cents C21.2:P27. Contains general information about trademarks and Patent Office. (See also C21.2:T67/960.)

Official Gazette of the Patent Office. Weekly. 300–400 pp. Subscription, $342.20 per year, C21.5; single copy $6.60.

Lists the patents, trade-marks, and design patents issued each week, and decisions of Commissioner of Patents and of United States courts in patent cases. Last weekly issue of each month includes a section entitled "Bulletin of Decisions of Patent Office on Trademarks."

Attorneys and Agents Licensed to Practice Before the U.S. Patent Office, C21.9/2 (Annual) $3.25. Geographical listings of individuals, with addresses.

Patents and Inventions. 25 pp., 40 cents. C21.2:P27/10. Explains importance of patents and summarizes six basic steps necessary to procure a patent. Discusses marketing and developing an invention.

Questions and Answers About Patents. 4 pp., free. Department of Commerce. Brief answers to twenty-eight questions about patents.

Questions and Answers About Trademarks. 4 pp., free. Department of Commerce. Brief answers to twenty-six common questions about trade-marks.

Daily Weather Map. $16.50 per year. C55.213. Consists of five maps, data for which are taken at different hours at hundreds of stations throughout North America. Includes data on temperature, precipitation, barometric pressure, and cloud type.

Business Service Checklist. Weekly. 4 pp. Subscription, $9.70 per year, C1.24; 25 cents a copy. Lists all materials published each week by U.S. Department of Commerce and selected publications of other agencies. News releases, books, pamphlets, reports, and other materials of interest to industry and business.

New Product Introduction for Small Business Owners, SBA 1.12:17, 90 cents. Provides basic information which will help the owners of small businesses understand better what is involved in placing a new or improved product on the market.

HOW TO REACH THE JAPANESE . . .

Possibly none of the subjects discussed is of interest to you. But you can be sure that ten minutes a month spent scanning the contents will turn up at least one lead that will spell dollars in your till. Let me give you a personal example.

I had a little item I felt would be good for the Japanese market. My problem was: how to reach the Japanese businessman? Advertise in the Tokyo papers? Which papers? What about the language barrier? I was mulling over the real problems and had just about given up the idea when an item in *Commerce Today* caught my eye. It led me to send for another publication, *World Trade List Catalog,* free, put out by the Bureau of International Commerce. We'll discuss this in more detail in Chapter IV. For present purposes, I learned that every industry in Japan has an "association," and every association puts out regular bulletins to its members, advising them of trade opportunities. There is no charge for getting your product described in these bulletins, provided it is of real or possible use to the Japanese businessmen who subscribe.

Now get this. *There are over sixty* of these associations in Japan. They cover every industry from silks to pharmaceuticals, from pearls to bicycles. In addition, there are Chamber of Commerce bulletins in the various cities listing many "trade opportunities." So, for the price of a mimeographed letter and sixty air mail stamps, I got my story before *five thousand* separate companies! I covered my expenses with the first order, and there were plenty more orders following the first.

STATISTICS ARE DOLLAR BILLS . . .

You're a functioning businessman, alert and eagerly perceptive to the ever-changing world we live in . . . and statistics are money in your pocket! If you don't believe me, take a look at Small Business Bibliography No. 12, *Statistics and Maps for National Market Analysis.* This is a brief, simplified introduction to a subject most people—quite wrongly—shy away from. It's a good starting point for newcomers to the field and a quick refresher for others.

Your Uncle Sam is the world's largest producer of statistics. You've heard of the five foot shelf? Well, a file of all government statistics would require literally miles of shelf space! Obviously, no one person needs or could use even a fraction of them. So, to help you find your way through this maze and to ferret out the figures, trends, and forecasts which will be meaningful to you, the Department of Commerce publishes several summaries. As an introduction to these summaries, this little SBB No. 12 is very useful. It brings statistics down to earth, as it were, by relating them directly to the businessman's problems. Giving actual pages from various statistical publications, the booklet shows you how to read statistics, how to understand them, and how to apply them to your own use. My guess is, after spending a half-hour with this free booklet, you'll never again look on statistics as dry stuff completely foreign to your business world. Let me tell you about three excellent publications on this subject.

> *Statistical Abstract of the United States.* This book covers a wide variety of subjects and contains over 1,100 tables. The *Abstract* is published yearly as a hard-cover, standard size book and is sold for $10.20 cloth, $6.85 paper by the Superintendent of Documents, Washington, D.C. 20402. In addition to selected statistics, the *Abstract* has a reference section for other sources of information. Because of its wide coverage, low price, and convenient size, the *Abstract* is the most useful single publication of government statistics.

County and City Data Book. For more local, geographic detail, the Department of Commerce publishes this volume. It presents a selection of available statistics for all counties and for cities of over 25,000 population. Priced at $18.80, it is published about once every three years and sold through the Superintendent of Documents, Washington, D.C. 20402.

Survey of Current Business. Monthly and quarterly statistics on a wide variety of subjects, but with no geographic detail, are published in this periodical. The yearly subscription is $48.30 for twelve issues, also from the Superintendent of Documents, Washington, D.C. 20402. In addition to varied and detailed information on income, production, prices, wages, employment, finance, foreign trade, and major industry groups (most of the data being shown month by month for the preceding year), each issue features articles on economic trends or other business subjects.

THE MEAT AND POTATOES . . .

Getting down to the meat of sales promotion, you could travel far and find less help than what's available in the Department of Commerce, Bureau of the Census Catalog. The price of this excellent quarterly catalog is $10.90 per year or $2.90 a single copy.

This periodical channels and summarizes market information in the form of brief descriptive paragraphs. The terse, fact-packed style is shown by these few excerpts from a single issue.

TC72-N *National Travel Survey* 1 Spring Travel, 96 pp. March 1973. $1.80. This report presents travel data for January through May 1972 for the nation, nine travel regions, and selected states. Data shown for number of persons taking trips, number of trips taken, person-trips, person-miles, and person-nights. Accommodations used are classified by such characteristics as means of transport, purpose of trip, duration, distance, size of party, vacation, and origin and destination. Data are also shown by such socioeconomic characteristics as residence, occupation, education, and family income level.

MA-35U *Vending Machines (Coin Operated): 1972* 4 pp. June 1973. Annual. 25¢. Subscription $1 per year. This report presents data on the shipment of vending machines (coin operated) in the United States during 1972. Tables show the value of shipments of coin-operated vending machines by product class for 1972, 1971, and 1967, with comparative data from the 1971 Annual Survey of Manufactures and the 1967 Census of Manufactures. For 1972 and 1971, statistics are presented on the quantity and value of shipments of coin-operated machines, including the number of companies reporting shipments of $100,000 or more, and the quantity and value of manufacturers' shipments, exports of domestic merchandise, and per cent exports to manufacturers' shipments. A statement on the limitations of comparing export, import, and output data has been included in the report.

MQ-35D *Construction Machinery* 9–12 pp. Quarterly. 25¢ per issue. Subscription price, $1 per year. Quarterly: Third quarter, fourth quarter 1972; First quarter, second quarter 1973. This report presents data for the United States on the quantity and value of total shipments and exports shown by type of equipment, for the current and preceding quarters. Included are data on contractors' off-highway wheel tractors; mixers, pavers, and related equipment; self-propelled ditchers and trenchers; water well and blast hole drills; and portable crushing plants, washing plants and combination plants.

These are government publications. However, just as helpful are works issued by private publishing houses; for example:

Accounting Systems for Management Control. Francis E. Moore and Howard F. Stettler. (Richard D. Irwin, Inc., 1818 Ridge Rd., Homewood, Ill.) 708 pp. $12.65. Discusses management information and control demands on the accounting system. Considers the basic elements of the accounting system and explains how these systems are developed in relationship to the various operating functions of business. Also covers professional aspects of accounting systems work—the design and installation of systems. Includes questions, problems, and cases.

Advertising Art International. (Modern Publicity Yearbook Number 32.) Hastings House, Publishers, 151 E. 50th St., New York 22, N.Y. Approx. 200 pp., 8½ × 11. $11.50. Reproductions (in black and white and color) of selected drawings and photographs used in advertising in U.S. and principal foreign countries. In each case indicates country, and media (or sub-class) in which illustration appeared. Introductory section discusses trends in modern advertising.

Guide to the Use of the Mails. Henry A. Berg. (Crane Press, Inc., 430 W. 16th St., New York 11, N.Y.) 49 pp. $2.00. Compact handbook of postal data to those who employ the mails in conducting business. Sections on classes of mail and types of postal service. Pinpoints specific regulations, as limited mailable and unmailable items, and postal meter machines. Well illustrated with drawings. Detailed index of contents.

Industrial Purchasing: Principles and Practices. Raymond R. Colton. (Charles E. Merrill Books, Inc., 1300 Alum Creek Dr., Columbus 16, Ohio.) 525 pp. $10.60. Provides fundamental information regarding procurement principles, procedures, and tools. Introduces established principles of purchasing and relates these principles to the specialized functions that have resulted from technological developments in the areas of materials, supplies, equipment, and services. In addition, gives attention to the specialized functions of scrap and waste recovery, expediting, scientific storage, value analysis, research, materials management, and traffic management.

Various publications of state and local Chambers of Commerce, university press publications, and other source material are likely to be useful to the man trying to market his products. Many college and university magazines are useful in marketing and economic research. Subscriptions to many of these are free, and others cost a few cents each. Here are a few, to give you an idea of this seldom tapped mine of valuable knowhow.

Boston University Monthly Index of Business Activity: New England and United States. Monthly. College of Business Administration, Boston University, Boston 15, Mass. 4 pp. Free.

Kansas Business Review. Monthly. Center for Research in Business, The University of Kansas, Lawrence, Kans. 16 pp. Free.

Mississippi's Business. Bimonthly. Bureau of Business and Economic Research, University of Mississippi, University, Miss. 6–8 pp. Free.

(Houston) The Business Review. Monthly. Center for Research in Business and Economics, University of Houston, Houston, Tex. 16 pp. $3 per year; 25 cents per single issue.

(Michigan) Business Topics. Quarterly. Bureau of Business and Economic Research, Graduate School of Business Administration, Michigan State University, East Lansing, Mich. 80 pp. On request to those concerned with business and economic matters.

Take another look at that offer from Michigan. *Eighty* pages of business reports, and absolutely free!

INTERESTED IN THE FOOD BUSINESS?

You can get dozens of merchandising aids that have been researched by the *Agricultural Research Service* of the U.S. Department of Agriculture. These reports are available from the Superintendent of Documents, Government Printing Office, Washington, D.C. 20402. Here are just a few of them. (Free unless price is given.)

Marketing Research Reports

Handling and Space Costs for Selected Food Wholesalers in Urban Distribution Centers
A1.82:992   40 cents
Methods and Equipment for Eviscerating Turkeys
A1.82:1006   55 cents
Consumer Preferences, Uses and Buying Practices for Selected Vegetables
A1.82:1019 $1.55
Standardization of Shipping Containers for Fresh Fruits and Vegetables
A1.82:991 $1.45
Waterproof Marine Ventilation System for Dry Freight Van Containers
A1.82:988   40 cents
Consumer Buying Practices, Uses and Preferences for Fibers in Retail Piece Goods
A1.82.1013   Free
Bin Fronts for Potato Storages   Free
Demand and Price Situation for Forest Products   Free
Rural Credit Program, Non-Farm Enterprises   Free

A KIT OF MARKETING TOOLS . . .

The Economic Development Administration of the Department of Commerce puts out a series of free booklets

under the general heading of *Urban Business Profile Series.*
These are especially geared to marketing and sales promotion, to help you to measure business potential.

The Area Redevelopment Act helps business to expand
and to establish in an area of poor employment. Naturally,
Uncle Sam is primarily interested in wiping out the blight of
unemployment and promoting the welfare of citizens every-
where. He feels, rightly, that one way to accomplish this is
through more and bigger markets for *your* business. And here
is the kind of aid the EDA is offering the businessman.

Economic Development Administration made available a specific kit of tools to help business establish or
expand in areas of chronic unemployment or underem-
ployment:

1. Low interest, long-term loans for new or expanding business firms.

2. Loans and grants to communities to help provide
public facilities needed if new firms are to be established
or existing firms expanded.

3. Technical assistance to help break barriers to economic growth.

4. Programs to help train jobless workers in new skills
required by an ever-changing industrial economy.

To these basic tools, the Area Redevelopment Administration has added a variety of other services to business and industry, including:

1. Information on redevelopment areas, labor force
and plant sites.

2. Studies of transportation, markets and sales.

3. One-stop service for businessmen seeking information on the programs of other federal departments and
agencies that will help in their expansion plans in redevelopment areas.

Your nearest U. S. Commerce Dept. Field Office will furnish you with information concerning the terms under which you can get a loan for business expansion, and a description of other services, etc.

The Social and Economic Statistics Administration of the U. S. Dept. of Commerce compiles Economic Censuses to provide you with the data from various economic areas. To aid your marketing, it is to your advantage to keep up with the latest trends in the business and industrial worlds. Study the material intelligently, and you'll be amazed at the opportunities to save money. Rather than costly experimentation, you'll get a bird's-eye view of your potential market in advance, helping you to lay out sensible territories for salesmen and to analyze their sales performance. You'll avoid expensive mistakes in locating plants, warehouses, and stores in the wrong places. Just a few examples show the practical uses of such reports for the businessman.

- A manufacturer who made a product for dairy farms used the census of agriculture to locate the counties with large numbers of dairy farms. He used the business census to see what kind of stores were in those areas to sell his products. When he sent salesmen out, he expected those who worked in the more prosperous areas to get more orders.

- In one instance, a businessman had an opportunity to invest in the manufacture of one-man haybalers. To determine the potential market, he obtained a special county-by-county tabulation of farms producing hay in quantity to justify purchase of such haybalers and then made his decision in favor of the investment. And, it proved to be a highly profitable operation; the census facts he needed to enter the undertaking cost him only a few hundred dollars.

- A recent case illustrates another use of Census

Bureau statistics in making a business decision. A large oil company was building a new refinery and considered building a plant that would make chemical fertilizer from a by-product of the refinery. The fertilizer plant would be profitable only if the company could sell its product nearby. The company determined the size of this potential market by examining such statistics as the size and number of farms in adjoining counties, the acreage in cropland, and the farm income.

• A department store which planned a suburban branch studied the suburban area carefully before it invested money. It found out how many other stores were in the area and how much business they did. It examined the population statistics to determine how many people lived there and whether another retail outlet was justified. Finally, it studied the people—particularly their incomes and personal characteristics—to decide what kinds of merchandise could be sold.

FOR THE MANUFACTURER . . .

My Cost 90 cents! My profit $25,000!

Take a look at the booklet published by the Small Business Administration: *New Product Introduction*. To help reduce your risk in this area, it answers such questions as:

1. How and where can I find ideas for new products?
2. How can my company improve its chances of selecting a successful new product?
3. How can I build a new product suitable to customer needs and desires?
4. How should name, package, and trade-mark be chosen?
5. What points should I consider in planning a marketing program for a new product?

Tips to help you reduce product failures "to almost zero": what are they worth to you? The SBA asks only 90 cents!

I credit this 90-cent book with a personal profit of $25,000. How? Someone had offered us a rather interesting gadget. It consisted of a plastic case about the size of this book, in which a spool of paper could be rolled backward and forward, something like the film in a camera. As the paper was exposed under a clear window, you could read the information on the scroll, a bit at a time.

As I originally saw it, the spool gave a series of drink recipes. I wasn't enchanted with the bartending aspect, feeling that it had a limited market. Furthermore, the experience of the patent holder hadn't been too promising. But I felt that this basic idea was a good one. Fresh from reading *New Product Introduction,* I set out to apply its principles toward making this little device saleable. (Just to show that no one is perfect, I must admit that I considered teaching information, such as spelling, simple arithmetic, and historical facts for little tots, and then discarded the idea. Five years later, teaching machines burst on the market full bloom and are, at this writing, a hot mail-order item!)

Convinced that if I filed my problem in the back of my head, the answer would come sooner or later, I bided my time and kept my eyes open. When the lightning struck, it was in a peculiar way. I was in a drugstore, fingering through a little booklet on first aid. Before my mind's eye flashed a page from *New Product Introduction.* I suddenly realized the type of information that would go best on my roller: first aid! Johnny cuts a finger, develops a fever, or falls off his bike. You want to know what to do, and you want to know fast. Zip through the little scroll for the answer! So I turned the product into an automated first-aid box called "Dial-Aid," took it to a large drug chain, and walked out with a clean, quick sale of the whole package, on an exclusive basis!

And talking about redesigning. . . . In *How I Made $1,000,000 in Mail Order,* I devoted a whole chapter to the ways in which we find our products. A section of that chapter counsels you to use the Government Publication Services. In a sense, this entire book is an outgrowth of that section, because, of course, I could only hit the highlights then. So you might say that this book, itself, is a case study of a product redesign!

HOW TO PUT YOUR SALESMEN WHERE THE MONEY IS . . .

Take a look at another booklet put out by the Office of Domestic Commerce. It's called *How Manufacturers Reduce Their Distribution Costs.* Here, for 45 cents, you get 150 pages of absolutely invaluable information of the kind that can make or break your business.

Taking the experiences of actual companies on the firing line, the book shows you how they cut their selling costs. You can follow their step-by-step planning and operation.

Once you've grasped the concept of profitable and unprofitable customers, it's easy for you to analyze your own customer list in this light and to cut out expensive selling cost wasted on those who don't bring you the profit to justify it.

And there are plenty more tips in this one pamphlet. How are your products sold? Through route sales, direct shipments, sales through wholesalers? You're shown how to analyze them for profit—again with illuminating examples from the files of actual firms. Orders, territories, salesmen's effort, routing, cost analysis, products, and physical distribution are carefully considered.

As a final example of Uncle Sam's continuing interest in your business welfare, let me point to SBA's Management Series No. 15, *A Handbook of Small Business Finance*. The foreword explains the purpose and scope of this highly popular 80-page pamphlet, which is yours for 30 cents. We quote:

> The objective of *A Handbook of Small Business Finance* is not to cover all phases of the subject. Nor is it to provide an exhaustive treatment of any one topic. Rather, it is to furnish new owners and inexperienced managers with basic information to help them understand better the financial operations of their businesses. As such, this booklet should aid businessmen in making better use of the financial assistance available to them—and particularly from local banks—guiding them in measuring the progress of their operations.

Financial statements, management, banking relationships, term loans, accounts receivable, and inventory financing are covered in the text. Chapter VI outlines some of the sources for financial assistance, through private venture capital organizations and industrial foundations. The SBA's own lending and investment programs are also discussed.

I have to remind you again, at the risk of repeating myself, that my effort here is *not* to cover the entire subject of help from the government. It would be impossible—physically impossible—to take a complete tour of Uncle Sam's five-mile bookshelf. But if I can give you an inkling of what's on that shelf, where to go for more—if I can impart some of my own enthusiasm and pride in this government that thinks enough of its citizens to go to this tremendous labor in their behalf—I'll have accomplished what I set out to do. All I can do is point to where the pay dirt is. All you have to do is grab a shovel and dig!

BIBLIOGRAPHY

Small Business Administration

A Handbook of Small Business Finance (Small Business
Management Series No. 15) 95¢

New Product Introduction for Small Business Owners
(Small Business Management Series No. 17) 90¢

Technology and Your New Product (Small Business Management Series No. 19) 75¢

Urban Business Profile Series   Free

Economic Development Administration, Commerce
Dept.

Survey of Consumer Buying Expectations P-65
C3.186:P65/44 Subscriptions GPO

Annual Survey of Manufactures C56.221/2:970–71 $6.60

Economic Censuses concerning:

    Retail Trade

    Wholesale Trade

    Selected Service Industries

    Construction Industries

    Enterprise Statistics

    Minority Owned Businesses

    Manufactures

    Minerals

    Transportation

(Free from: Subscriber Services Section (Publications)
               Social and Economic Statistics Admin.
               Washington, D. C. 20233

CHAPTER IV

UNCLE SAM AS YOUR OVERSEAS ASSISTANT

The World—Your Oyster—
with Government Help

Be glad you're doing business today instead of in the days before World War I. That war marked the end of an era for the United States, a period during which we distrusted and discouraged foreign trade. Later, the high tariff walls came tumbling down, and we learned that the world outside our borders was a great big market, hungry for goods with the "Made in U.S.A." stamp and ready to pay good prices for them.

To see how startlingly different things are today, all you have to do is glance through a slim blue leaflet put out by the Field Services of the Bureau of International Commerce, entitled *Export Information Services Available for U. S. Business Firms.* * It's a real eye-opener. Just listen:

Let Your Field Office Help You Research Foreign Markets. Market research probably is even more important in foreign selling than in domestic. Trained business

*The Bureau of International Commerce was formerly called the Bureau of Foreign Commerce, which accounts for the titles on some older publications. However, your inquiry to either will reach the Bureau.

analysts in the Department's Field Offices will assist you in making a market analysis. With the aid of their extensive files and new data received daily, they will:

Help you determine which foreign countries are the best customers for your firm's products . . .

Tell you about the foreign country's import tariffs and import and exchange controls as they apply to your products . . .

Lend you copies of detailed descriptions of market conditions in the country of interest . . .

Furnish detailed current information on economic conditions in the country of interest . . .

Arrange for you to consult with Bureau of International Commerce* country specialists in Washington, if necessary. These specialists are highly trained international economists who concentrate on one or two countries and can answer most of your questions quickly and completely.

How the BIC Helps You to Contact Foreign Firms Interested in Buying Your Products. The periodical *Commerce Today* regularly carries reports of specific foreign businessmen who have visited our Embassies and Consulates to ask about buying specific U.S. products.

World Trade List Catalog, free from the Bureau of International Commerce, lists reliable, significant foreign firms engaged in the import business.

Trade Contact Surveys are quick, efficient methods of finding reliable and aggressive sales agents and distributors in foreign countries. At your request, experienced Foreign Service officers canvass particular foreign cities and report at least three companies which meet your requirements.

World Trade Data Reports are valuable and they are available on any firm in any free world country. Prepared by the *Export Information Division,* they describe the operations of the company and list products handled, manufacturers from whom it imports, size and reputation of the company, its capital and annual turnover, and other important facts.

Information about purchases being made by foreign firms and governments under Agency for International Development (AID) foreign aid programs is disseminated by Field Offices.

If you have agents abroad, the Agency Index may assist you. This service, maintained by our Embassies and Consulates, lists names and addresses of local companies which carry products of specific U.S. Manufacturers. From this list, FS posts can direct other local businessmen to your agent.

And, as usual, Uncle Sam, your export assistant, is ready to flood you with more help and information.

There are several sources of clear, concise information about the necessary paperwork of overseas shipments:

World Trade Information Service reports entitled "Preparing Shipments to (country)" are available on most countries. Field Offices have supplementary information about the documents you need for any shipment to any country.

Special counseling and publications on techniques of shipping, such as the roles of freight forwarders, carriers, insurance companies, custom house brokers, banks, and others, and on export control regulations and procedures for securing necessary export licenses may be obtained at any Field Office.

Field Offices can supply all Department of Commerce forms needed in foreign trade and will assist you in completing them correctly.

Obviously, Uncle Sam is in two-way foreign trade with both feet and is ready to knock himself out to give you the benefit of it all. What does this mean? Well, as I see it, it means you can count your potential customers not in the thousands, or even millions . . . but in the *billions!*

In an earlier book of mine, *How I Made $1,000,000 in Mail Order,* published by Prentice-Hall, Inc., I brought out some pertinent points about selling overseas. While that book was directed to the mail-order business, the pointers are just as important for you, whether you manufacture or distribute and whether or not you consider yourself a mail-order firm.

I said in that book:

> Especially today—because of the Common Market— many of you should give a good deal of thought to overseas sales. And what is the "Common Market"? The Common Market is literally a "United States of Europe" that originally consisted of France, West Germany, Italy, The Netherlands, Belgium and Luxemburg. These countries formed a single economic union to serve 170 million European consumers and its success is beyond all expectations. Although the Common Market is only a few years old, by the end of 1961 all quota restrictions on trade in industrial goods between the six countries had been established, and before long it appears that merchandise will be able to move freely from one Common Market country to another without being hampered by tariffs, taxes or duties. The ultimate aim is to unite most of the European countries into a European Economic Federation with a total of 250 million people whose products and workers will be able to move as freely across the national borders as we move across state borders in the United States.
>
> Now is the time to get your product distributed in these Common Market countries and the working tools described in this chapter can help you achieve this goal. To many people the foreign market seems remote and

mysterious, but once you learn a few basic marketing tricks, it's sometimes almost easier to sell ten thousand units of your product to an importer in Milan, Italy than ten dozen to a jobber in Chicago. Quite often the same qualities that sell your product in the U.S.A. will also find a ready and willing market overseas. People are basically the same throughout the world . . . usually what appeals to an American father, mother and child, or average consumer will strike a responsive chord in their overseas counterpart.

In that chapter I went on to touch on many of the government sources of help we'll go over more fully here. And the help is so unusually rich, it's hard to know where to begin. Maybe a personal experience will show you one way that this tremendous market can be tapped.

A case in point is our Cossman Fly Cake. Fly Cake is a solid chemical, in the shape of a small doughnut, with the incredible ability to kill flies a few seconds after they touch the cake. Best of all, Cossman Fly Cake retains its killing power for an entire season and is effective as long as a single crumb remains. Because of these remarkable qualities, Fly Cake easily found a place in the American market, and we soon began searching for other markets overseas.

Aside from a one-time experience in export selling several years ago, we had no previous background in this field. We were fortunate in selling 200,000 Cossman Fly Cakes to an organization in Australia, and this whetted our appetite for more of this lucrative business. One thing amazed us: the 200,000 Cossman Fly Cake order from Australia was no more complicated than selling a few gross to any one of our jobber accounts here in the United States. So, what did we do to get more of this foreign business? We contacted the Bureau of International Commerce in Washington, D.C., and asked their advice on how to get overseas agents for our products. The bureau referred us to their office in Los Angeles, and we couldn't believe our eyes when we made our first call there. The local Los Angeles office was a merchandising wonderland of ideas on how to get business overseas. Today, Cossman Fly Cake is sold in most of the major countries throughout the world, and I can truthfully say that a good part of our success in our world-wide distribution of Fly Cake is due to the help and assistance we received from the Department of Commerce. Let me tell you about a few of these services.

ACTIONS SPEAK LOUDER . . .

I've won many a drink from a smart businessman by betting him he couldn't name five of the actual pavement-pounding services the government offers the overseas trader. Can you?

Pick up a booklet called *Fourteen Ways the U. S. Department of Commerce Can Help Make Your Business More Profitable* and note the many services available to you. (Incidentally, unless otherwise noted all references in this chapter are published by and available from the Bureau of International Commerce, which is part of the Department of Commerce; unless prices are quoted, they are free. Write to the Commerce Field Office nearest you. The list is in Chapter I.)

1. Need a Consulting Service?

Specialists in the Bureau of International Commerce cover most foreign countries on economic developments, regulations you'll have to follow, trade statistics, etc. Even old-timers in the field have plenty of need for these Bureau of International Commerce specialists, and a newcomer will find them a lifesaver. They help you to complete your picture of any country as far as buying your products is concerned, and they give you straight, factual answers to specific questions. It's almost like having high-ranking, top-level consulting specialists on your payroll—free.

2. Uncle Knocks on Doors for You

How'd you like a top American businessman—say the president of U.S. Steel or Xerox, or Continental Can—to go to work for *you* . . . for *free?* Pipe dreams? Ordinarily, yes. But wouldn't it be loverly?

All right, you can wake up . . . and it's true. Every year United States trade missions carry thousands of queries from American businessmen to foreign countries. The answers they bring back have helped many companies to find overseas markets for their products. These trade missions are actually top-level private business executives, working with government officials, who volunteer their services to promote United States trade abroad. They conduct on-the-spot discussions with foreign businessmen and find out exactly what they need and want. Each year twelve to fifteen of these missions visit twenty or more countries. Think what it would cost you to send a high-salaried, experienced representative to each of these twenty countries to find out whether it's worth-while for you to make a pitch to that country for *your* products! Uncle Sam does all this spadework for the cost to you of a ten-cent stamp!

HERE'S HOW IT WORKS. Let's say you're a toy manufacturer looking for new markets in foreign countries. First, check with your local Department of Commerce Field Office for countries scheduled for trade missions. Then answer the following nine questions by letter sent to your Field Office. (Where more than one country is scheduled there should be one original and two carbon copies of your letter for each foreign country).

1. Do you now have business connections or are you represented in any of these countries? (If you have an exclusive representative, the trade mission cannot locate another agent for you.) If you are represented, by whom and in which country (countries)?

2. Have you had previous business experience with these countries? List countries.

3. What products do you wish to sell or purchase and in which countries? Or, what type of business transactions do you wish to make? Describe products in detail.

4. Do you wish to obtain an agent or do you prefer to export directly? If so, in which countries?

5. Do you prefer to import for your own account or to act as an agent?

6. Will you consider direct investment or a joint venture, such as providing machinery, know-how, or capital with a qualified firm?

7. Are you interested in licensing a qualified company to produce your products abroad? If so, describe in detail the nature of the agreement you would consider.

8. To what extent are you prepared to sell on long-term credit or, if dollar exchange is not available, accept payment in foreign currency?

9. What type of company would be qualified to transact your business?

Whatever pertinent information a company can provide will help the agents of the trade mission. This includes catalogues and brochures as well as information about the size and scope of a company's activities. No one is too large or too small to be represented.

When the trade mission get to the country in question, they will explore the market potential for you and scout for profitable export-import opportunities, agents or distributors, licensing possibilities, etc. And all this costs you the grand sum of a *ten-cent* postage stamp. How can you beat it?

On the other side of the coin, the trade mission will also look for trade opportunities for you in the country they visit. For example, let's assume you wanted to represent a good perfume manufacturer from France. You would contact the trade mission leaving for France, tell them of your wishes, and when they get to France, they would literally knock on doors to locate a good company for you.

3. Uncle's Date Bureau

This is the reverse of the foreign-trade mission. Responsible businessmen from other countries visiting the United States are invited to come to the Department of Commerce and use its facilities. Their names, firms, purpose of visit, time and place to contact them—all these are printed in *Commerce Today*. So you can contact these businessmen from foreign lands without the expense of a business trip.

4. Unaccustomed as I Am

Maybe you can't speak on your feet, but the Bureau of International Commerce does it for you. The Bureau of International Commerce is the businessman's voice in the development of American foreign-trade policy. Both at home and abroad, bureau officials set forth the views of American world traders and help to promote their best interests. The bureau works to improve the world climate for American capital by co-operating with other countries and tearing down obstacles to investment. Tariffs, export and import controls, transportation, communications, utilities, currency, property rights, customs regulations, insurance, loans and investment, arbitration of trade disputes—these are the areas in which the bureau is your world spokesman.

5. Want a Foreign Agent?

Not the cloak-and-dagger type, of course, but a representative for your product abroad. A special service in your field is available to help you find agents or distributors in foreign countries to sell your products. If you have been unable to make satisfactory trade connections through regular sources of information supplied by the Bureau of International Commerce—World Trade List Catalog, International Marketing Information, Commerce Today, and other media —you may apply for a Trade Contact Survey.

WHAT THE SERVICE IS. A Trade Contact Survey is a specialized, professional service designed to locate several foreign firms in a particular country which meet your specific requirements and which express an interest in the representation you offer. It is conducted "on the spot' by a Foreign Service officer at the request of BIC.

TIME REQUIRED. A survey is usually completed in about sixty days. The time is subject to difficulty encountered in locating suitable prospects but an interim report will be supplied.

RESULTS OF SURVEY. You will receive a summary report of the information developed, including pertinent marketing data as well as the names and addresses of qualified prospects. Individual World Trade Data reports giving background information on these firms are also furnished. If the Foreign Service officer has been unable to locate any firms interested in the proposal or if the particular operation planned is not feasible the reasons will be explained in the report and possible alternate suggestions offered.

PRICE. A charge of $10.00 is made for each survey conducted.

HOW TO APPLY. Ask the Department of Commerce Field Office in your area to supply you with copies of form FC-963, Application for Assistance in Selecting an Agent or Distributor Abroad. Members of the Field Office staff will also assist you in preparing the forms. Or you may write to the Export Information Division, Room 1313, Bureau of International Commerce, U. S. Department of Commerce, Washington, D. C. 20230.

There are the five services to win the bet. But we haven't begun to tap Uncle's capacity to help! Let's look at a few more.

6. Need a Mailing List of Prospective Foreign Customers?

The World Trade List Catalog identifies firms handling specific commodities in foreign countries, and covers a wide range of products, trades and services.

7. Want to Draw a Credit Report on a Foreign Company?

World Trade Data Reports contain business particulars on individual foreign firms. These reports, which complement the trade list service, supply the detailed information needed to determine the competence and general reliability of specific foreign firms. They are prepared by the American Foreign Service and represent a consensus of reliable sources of information. If the report on file is more than a year old, a revised current report is prepared without additional charge. The complete name and address of the foreign firm should be given when ordering World Trade Data Reports. These reports cost only $15.00 each.

8. Looking for a Foreign Advertising Agency?

One of the best sources of information is the Department of Commerce's book entitled *A Directory of Foreign Advertising Agencies and Marketing Research Organizations*. This *Directory* costs only 45 cents but is worth many, many times that amount. It gives detailed information on advertising agencies and marketing research organizations in most of the civilized countries of the world.

9. Want a List of Foreign Business Directories?

Again, contact your Department of Commerce and buy their book, *A Guide to Foreign Business Directories.* This *Guide* is intended for businessmen seeking to identify persons or companies engaging in commerce, a specific industry, or a profession in other countries. The *Guide* is presented in two principal parts:

(a) The first part, *Country Directories,* contains the titles of directories published in or dealing with countries of the free world. These countries are arranged alphabetically.

(b) The second principal part of the *Guide* lists directories alphabetically by industry, trade, or profession. Here in one volume you'll find information on directories of importers, manufacturers, suppliers, exporters, trade associations, individual professional and businessmen, and government officials. It also gives you the names and addresses of each directory's publisher, where to get the directory, and the price.

10. A Little Bit of Home

If you import or export, or even manufacture an article using a foreign part or ingredient, you'll do well to look into the little-known "Free Port" or Foreign Trading Zone system. These ports are spotted all over the trading world. American vacationers who have stopped at the famous Shannon free port where Irish whisky can be bought without paying duty can testify to at least one of these benefits! The United States has six of these ports: at Staten Island, Seattle, New Orleans, Toledo, San Francisco, and one in Puerto Rico.

More and more, businessmen are becoming aware of the advantages of the system. A small manufacturer unable to afford overseas facilities otherwise can now use the ports as a money-saving alternative. The Foreign Trade Zones Board publishes a booklet you can get for 30 cents, entitled *Laws, Regulation, and Other Information Relating to Foreign Trade Zones in the United States.* Unfortunately, the text is just as stuffy as the title, but it's worth the effort of reading when thousands of dollars may be saved by understanding what it has to say. The basic idea of the free port is that goods deposited or manufactured in the free-port area are technically not considered to have entered the United States and are therefore not subject to import duty unless and until they actually cross into the United States proper. The booklet also explains some of the other free-port privileges.

A beautiful provision of the system is that you pay duty only on the merchandise "weight" actually imported. Taking advantage of this, a friend of mine saved $20,000 on a shipment of Brazil nuts. The unripe nuts waited in the Staten Island port for several months while the moisture content dropped from 50 per cent to less than 10 per cent. Thus, he was spared paying up to a cent and a half a pound for pure water! This is watering the stock, in reverse!

TRAVEL IS BIG BUSINESS . . .

The Department of Commerce has the job, among many others, of promoting tourist trade. Naturally, the travel industry is delighted to co-operate. Other countries are encouraged to let down bars that hamper the travel of Americans abroad, and we likewise encourage visits by foreign vacationers. In recent years you see more and more advertisements and posters in European countries, inviting Frenchmen, Englishmen, Italians, etc., to visit the Grand Canyon and Disneyland. This traffic is on the increase and every visitor is a potential customer. Maybe for you!

THE WATER'S FINE! . . .

Have I convinced you that Uncle Sam doesn't stop with the printed word when it comes to helping you do business overseas? That doesn't mean that he's shy on literature in this field. So let's take a look at some of the publications you can get on foreign trade.

As a starter, go back to the book we quoted in the preceding chapter, the *Directory of Foreign Organizations.* The free publicity you can get for appropriate trade notices and inquiries is fantastic. For instance, if you have something to interest English businessmen, you can reach 26,500 British firms with a *free* notice by sending it to just *three* journals! That's the combined membership of the London Chamber of Commerce monthly *Commerce,* the *FBI Journal* (of the Federation of British Industries), and the *British Manufacturer.* Similar opportunities are open in many other countries. Consult the *Directory* for the nation you are interested in.

If you've never looked into import-export, you can get the full story in the handbook put out by the Foreign Commerce Department of the Chamber of Commerce, Washington 6, D.C. It's called Basic Guide to Exporting. It costs $2.00 and is worth a thousand times the price. While not a government agency, the Chamber of Commerce is of course the next thing to one and gives you the same full, impartial, and objective kind of service. This 136-page book takes up importing and exporting and each of the topics is fleshed out in detail. For instance the subheadings on the chapter entitled "the Import Order" include:

> Essential Considerations.
> The Quotation: Price, Currency of Quotation, Weights and Measures, Quality Guarantees, Foreign Trade Definitions, Method of Payment.

Other Terms of Purchase.
Arbitration.
Packing.
Marking.
Import Documents.
   Invoices
   Statement of Charges
   Packing List
   Inspection of Analysis Certificate
   Bill of Lading
   Insurance Policy
Forwarding of Documents.

I have found this book handy for quick reference on all my own overseas transactions.

For the government treatment of the over-all picture, turn to *Guides for the Newcomer to World Trade,* published by the BIC for 15 cents. It is especially valuable in referring you to other publications put out by the BIC and the Bureau of Domestic Commerce. The specialists in this BDSA gather, sift, and pass out information on the commercial activity in many specific industries. Here are some of the subscriptions you can order.

Rubber. Monthly. $1.75 a year. Presents production trends, sales, inventories, outlook for selected commodities, foreign developments, and special analyses of specific chemical and rubber products.

Containers and Packaging. Quarterly. $2.00 a year. Reviews current and near-future trends of these industries. Contains analyses and all data on production, consumption, inventories, exports, imports, and current and future trends and includes occasional special articles on foreign markets for packaging materials and equipment.

Copper. Quarterly. $2.00 a year. Presents statistical data and analyses covering such subjects as requirements for and distribution of copper-base raw materials as well as for mill and foundry products, exports and imports of copper, and shipments and unfulfilled orders of brass mill and copper wire mill products.

Pulp, Paper and Board. Quarterly. $2.00 a year. Reviews current and future trends, sales, inventories, wholesale distribution, employment, prices, and other related factors.

Foreign trade participation by the Department of State, Department of Agriculture, the Customs Bureau, Food and Drug Administration, and others are also covered in this booklet. But before we leave BDSA, we should mention that this bureau also publishes a general information booklet by the title of *What You Should Know about Exporting.* The cost is 25 cents. In addition, you can get books on specific areas, such as *The Market for Automatic Vending Machines in Austria* (25 cents) and *Electric Current Abroad* (also 25 cents).

For more detail and background information, the BIC publishes a *Checklist of BFC Publications.* It's free for the asking, and the most recent issue will contain up-to-the-minute trade reports that can be obtained from more than 290 Foreign Service Posts throughout the world. The trade reports and market research are analyzed, correlated, and supplemented by BIC's own specialists.

Listing the most current and useful books and pamphlets, the *Checklist* gives information on all phases of market research data for foreign trade. Here are a few examples.

Information Sources on International Travel. Twelve mimeographed listings of basic source material for use by the international travel industry and the general traveling public. Check list and order form available from U.S. Department of Commerce, Washington 25, D.C., and its Field Offices.

Investment Handbooks. A series designed to assist both exporters and investors in marketing abroad. Describes basic conditions and economic outlook for a particular country, giving comprehensive data on the country's natural resources, industry, transport, communications, power facilities, finance, taxation, business methods, and trade, and the government's attitude toward private foreign investment.

Seasonal Patterns of United States Travel Abroad. An analysis of quarterly periods of United States overseas travel. Presents detailed information on number of travelers (for specific years), purpose, means of transportation, and other travel factors for selected aeas. 54 pages. 20 cents.

Sending Gift Packages. Nearly every country in the world is covered in this series of circulars describing United States and foreign country regulations on what can be included in a gift package, what senders should know about packaging regulations, what the recipient must do to receive gift packages, and what he must pay. Available from the United States Department of Commerce, Washington 25, D.C., and its Field Offices. 10 cents per country report.

Sources of Credit Information on Foreign Firms. A guide to reference sources of foreign credit information in the United States and abroad. 84 pages. 30 cents.

Sources of Information on Foreign Trade Practice. A guide to the principal reference sources giving the exporter and importer fundamental information on foreign-trade techniques. 47 pages. 25 cents.

Survey of International Travel. Assembles basic facts and figures about the United States' share in the growing business of international travel. Traces the pattern and expenditures for travel since such statistics were first recorded by the United States Government. Includes a list of foreign tourist information offices in the United States and selected references. 63 pages. 35 cents.

After all this, the booklet takes up more than a hundred nations, country by country, showing the material you can receive on each one.

Another booklet to guide you through the profitable foreign-trade maze is: *Export Marketing for Smaller Firms* ($1.30). This booklet lists Government publications as well as other titles from public and private sources.

The BIC also publishes that wonderful periodical, *Commerce Today*. This weekly magazine offers practical, authoritative, and concise international marketing information and news and reports demonstrating and explaining potential advantages to American businessmen in profitable international sales of United States products around the world, in the easily read form of a weekly news magazine. It carries feature articles on significant developments in the United States export trade expansion and other programs, the accomplishments of United States trade missions, analyses of United States and foreign trade, and reports on outstanding activities of such organizations as GATT, the Common Market, Eximbank, the World Bank, ECAFE, and ECSC. (Annual subscription: $54.05, $13.55 additional for foreign mailing). Make your remittance payable to the Superintendent of Documents and mail either to a Department of Commerce Field Office or to the Superintendent of Documents, U.S. Government Printing Office, Washington, D.C., 20402. A single copy is free as a sample; otherwise single copies cost $2.10.

Articles by experts are sandwiched between opportunity tips on world trade. For example, the issue open in front of me contains a special report on seven hundred trade fairs being held in sixty-one countries whose doors are open to American exhibitors and vendors. Business outlook articles and the latest word on government actions here and abroad fill out the publication. Here is part of the table of contents of a recent issue:

SPECIAL REPORTS—East Africa: a Common Market
Open to U.S. Goods.
Features
Hearings Underway on Items for GATT Negotiations
Neil Hurley's Column
'E' Award Winners Near Total of 400
Trade Fairs and Centers
Household Goods Show Scheduled in Cologne
Specialized Hotel Equipment Fair to Be Held in Paris
Worldwide Business Outlook
Wave of Optimism Carries Ecuador's Economy
Venezuelan Upturn Continues Despite Pre-election
Lull
U.S. Government Actions
California, Chile form Partnership under Alliance
Foreign Government Actions
Syria Imposes More Taxes on Imported Cinema Films
Investment Opportunities
Final East African List Shows Area's Great Potential
Private Aid Sought for Pakistan Projects
World Trade Opportunities
Variety of Equipment Sought in Several Countries
New Trade Lists; Visiting Buyers and Officials
Leads for Exporters
Special Trade Leads
International Representation
Leads for Importers
Construction Projects

As a sample of the very usable information you may
expect to find between these covers, a recent article headed
"Interest of U.S. Exporters in Swedish Textile Market Picks
Up" by the commercial attaché at Stockholm, Mr. Gustave
E. Larson, sent a friend of mine racing to get more information about selling his line of sports clothes in Sweden, an idea
that had never occurred to him before. He got all the information he needed through a trade mission and was put in

touch with a responsible firm willing and anxious to act as his Swedish distributor. A year later he racked up over a quarter-million dollars in sales from this unexpected market, which also led him to many other European countries as potential customers.

THE RED CARPET . . .

There's a big dessert at the end of this foreign-trade banquet sponsored, hosted, and catered by your Uncle Sam. It's this: If you really jump into the big foreign market, sooner or later you'll find yourself traveling to some of the countries where you've done business or corresponded. In my book, *How I Made $1,000,000 in Mail Order,* I told how I was wined, dined, and treated like royalty on my first trip over, driven around in Rolls-Royces, introduced to the biggest business tycoons . . . and all through the contacts made with the help of the BIC and the other agencies I've been beating the drum about throughout this chapter. It can happen to you, too! It doesn't matter if your office is a hole in the wall or a corner of your kitchen table; the foreign contacts are made through your impressive letterhead, and for all that your business friends abroad know, you could buy and sell General Motors three times a day. What's the moral? Simply this: *You don't have to be a big man to do big business!*

All right. Fifteen billion dollars worth of goods are sold abroad annually by American businessmen. Get busy and grab *your* share!

BIBLIOGRAPHY

Source: Dept. of Commerce
   Overseas Trade Promotion Calendar free
   Export Mailing List and FTI Data Tape Services free
   U.S. Trade Promotion Facilities Abroad free

Selected Publications to Aid Domestic Business and Industry free

Wholesale Data Sources for Market Analysis free

Obtain Tax Referral Through International Sales Corporation free

Export Information Services for U. S. Business Firms free

Brazil, A Survey of U. S. Export Opportunities free

Fourteen Ways the U. S. Dept of Commerce Can Help Make your Business More Profitable free

Overseas Private Investment Corporation

International Economic Indicators (qrtly) free

Handbooks on

    Investment

    Insurance

    Investment Financing

    Construction Industries

    Small Business

    Cooperative and Financial Institutions

Source: U. S. Government Printing Office

Source of Information On American Firms for International Buyers 30 cents

Electric Current Abroad 85 cents

Commerce Today (Biweekly) C1.58

Subscription $54.05 per year, single copies $2.10

Overseas Business Reports C1.50

Subscription $28.50 per year, single copies 30 cents

Foreign Service List (triannually) S1.7

Subscription $6.50 per year, single copies $2.25

Key Officers in Foreign Posts, A Guide for Businessmen S1.40/2:Of 2 (triannually)

Subscription $3.00 per year, single copies $1.00

Foreign Consular Offices (Annual) S1.69:974 $1.15

Foreign Economic Trends and Their Implications for the U.S.

C42.30 Subscription $37.50 per year

Single copies from the Department of Commerce Field Offices

CHAPTER V

UNCLE SAM AS YOUR IDEA MAN

INCREASING YOUR PROFITS
WITH GOVERNMENT HELP

Next to your wife, there's no one more anxious to see you get ahead in your business than that Uncle of yours. He has a million ideas for you to use and is begging you to take them, free. Let's look into some of the tricks he has up his sleeve to increase your profits.

WOULD YOU LIKE FREE USE OF A GOVERNMENT OWNED INVENTION?

You are welcome to it. That's right: the patented ideas of hundreds of thousands of inventors are all yours for the asking. The patents belong to the government, which asks no royalty from you.

Where does this free bonanza come from? Well, many are patents and processes and products developed by the government itself, through its many research laboratories. If General Electric or Remington-Rand had developed the ideas, they'd belong to the proper corporations and would be out of your reach. But because the government scientists created them, they're offered to you on a royalty-free license.

Other patents are "dedicated," that is, given to the government by civic-minded business firms and individuals. We learn that when a patent is dedicated the inventor gives up all ownership and control of the invention. Therefore, no license to make, use or sell the invention is required, and no royalty need be paid.

Just to cite a few important products originating through government research and development: There's the remote control for television sets (which came as a result of remote control command systems for missiles and satellites); also the electronic wrist watch. Of course, you don't get exclusive use; anyone else is free to take up the same idea. Chances are, however, that he'll use it differently and in a way that doesn't compete with you. That's because most of the ideas need imagination and initiative to make them commercial. Few of these patents are ready for the market "as is," but a little engineering work and a lot of sales know-how will develop many of them into profitable products to add to your own line.

These ideas are briefly described in the free Patent Abstract Series, published by the Office of Technical Services, Department of Commerce. This is a series of publications designed to inform the business public of patented inventions owned by the government which are ordinarily available for license to private firms on a royalty-free basis. Many small and large companies are now manufacturing products or using processes covered by government owned patents or developed through further engineering work based on such government patents.

Reading a few of the different items listed in these books will give you some idea of the sales possibilities opened up in this idea grab bag. They cover toys, sporting goods, athletic supplies, pens, pencils, costume jewelry, novelties and notions, clocks and watches—to name only a few. In one of these lists, we found an improved earphone-socket design which we adapted and sold to television, radio, and tape-recorder listeners at a nice profit.

If you want more information about any of the inventions, you can get the complete specifications and claims made for the device or process for 25 cents from the Commissioner of Patents, Department of Commerce. And when you decide to use one of the inventions, you apply to the government agency which is listed as administrator of the patent. This will usually be one of the Cabinet Departments (Commerce, Defense, or Agriculture), but in some cases it may be administered by the Tennessee Valley Authority, the Atomic Energy Commission, GSA, or the Federal Power Commission.

MORE PATENTS . . . BUT NOT FREE . . .

While we're on the subject of patents, we must not forget the 1,200 patents that are granted *each week* to inventors. We'll talk about how you can secure a patent on a device or process of your own invention later in this book. Here, I want to talk about other people's patents. Every one of them, of course, was patented in the fervent hope that you or some other businessman would offer to buy, rent, or pay a royalty on it. These new patents are described as they come out in the Patent Office's weekly *Official Gazette.* Besides describing newly granted patents (with illustrations), it lists patents available for licensing or sale, reports news of patent suits, lists new trade-mark registrations, and gives other information you may want to know about. Your local library probably has a copy. If 1,200 patents a week seems like a lot, remember the two fellows who looked out over the ocean. "Big, ain't it?" said one. "Sure is," said the other, "and you're only seeing the top of it!"

The new patents you see listed in the *Official Gazette* are only the surface of the literally millions of patents available. To read about these, you'll have to go to the Patent Office in Washington or to one of the depository libraries in a number of larger cities. (The Patent Office in Washington or your own public library will tell you where the nearest one is located.)

A personal experience will give you an idea of the value of this ocean of business opportunities. After an evening at the symphony, watching the players turn pages of music, I thought that there might be a market for an automatic page turner to be used by musicians. At the patent room of the Los Angeles Public Library an obliging clerk helped me run down inventions already patented. There were a dozen or more. Many of them were so complicated that it would be impossible to make them, much less sell them; but I did find one that was light and simple and looked as if it could be brought in at a realistic price. I got in touch with the inventor, who had had no luck in merchandising his invention. He'd made a stab at selling his baby and had got nowhere. I made a deal for his tooling, putting him on a royalty. Advertising in the music magazines, we sold 12,000 of the devices at $7.95, making both the inventor and me quite happy.

The moral is: if you need a product not yet on the market, don't assume there is no such thing. Try the resources of the Patent Office first.

STILL MORE PATENTS . . .

Just one last word on another little known source of *free* ideas. That's the storehouse of over 100,000 different items of technical know-how our government acquired as war reparations from German and Japanese laboratory and factory records and enemy owned patents. Added to this are some of the results of United States wartime research that have been opened to public use without charge. Write to the Office of Technical Services for information on this free bonanza of ideas.

I recently developed and am now manufacturing a plastic frogman that swims under its own power for thirty minutes or more on a single fuel pellet. And where did I find the pellet? In a German patent that our government acquired after World War II! The patent gave details about a harmless chemical that created a steady stream of carbon dioxide when mixed with water. We merely took the formula, combined it into a small fuel pellet, and it will soon be propelling our plastic frogman into one of the top toy products in the country today . . . and our total development cost for the fuel propellent was a letter to the Office of Technical Services! Incidentally, we also used this same formula in a fishing lure that swims under its own power for one hour or more, and which became another one of our winners!

A *last* word on patents: A publication called *Products List Circular* put out monthly by the SBA (free), lists not only privately owned and government owned patents but also those patents which are expiring at the end of their 14- or 28-year period—your chance to pick up an invention in "public domain" which you will not have to buy or lease but may use absolutely free. To save you from wading through a lot of useless material, the Small Business Administration selects the patents which have the most commercial possibilities. Many gift and giveaway items are featured. Here are some typical products from one issue:

Antenna Clip	Fastening Device
Cabinet Support	Headset

Ear Pads
Battery-Charging System
Door Latch
Electric Fence Post
Eraser Cleaner
Receptacle for Lipstick
  Holders and Lipsticks
Screen for Picture Projection
Skirt Rack
Baby Bottle Holder
Collapsible Pet Animal House
Fishing Implement

Automobile Headlight
  Control Devices
Folding Flashlight Holder
Fishing-Rod Holder
Combination Toilet Tissue
  Roll and Deodorant
  Container
Rodent Exterminator
Inflatable Hat
Razor Blade Holder
Cigarette Holder
Hide-A-Way Door Stop

GOVERNMENT RESEARCH AT YOUR FINGERTIPS . . .

The creative thinking of the nation is piled up not only in patents but in research, and much of it belonging to the government is yours to use. An annual subscription to Weekly Government Abstracts, which covers various subjects, will give you access to government reports on products, processes, and investigations that may be useful to your business.

Most of these reports are highly technical. But even a layman can understand the importance of an Army Medical Research Study on the digestibility and acceptability of a new dehydrated ration. Maybe this item, under a name like "Fruit-Flakies," could be the next blockbuster in the breakfast food industry! But certainly, if you have anything to do with electronics, machinery, medicine, photography, or transportation, there may be something here for you.

Remember the Management Aids? We discussed them earlier in Chapters I and II as tools to choose and build a business. Let's pull out the list again and go over the titles once more, this time thinking of them as a *source of ideas*. Here are a few titles right off the top of the pile.

Know Your Patenting Procedures
Getting Your Product on a Qualified Products List
Wishing Won't Get Profitable New Products
Publicize Your Company by Sharing Information
Expanding Sales Through Franchising
Using Census Data in Small Plant Marketing
Expand Overseas Sales with Commerce Department Help

If I haven't already mentioned it, you can get a complete list of titles with order blanks from the SBA without cost. Before leaving this series, I want to suggest that you especially look into SBA Management Series pamphlet No. 25, *Guides for Profit Planning* (70 cents). It helps you decide whether your earnings and profits are reasonable in your present situation. If they are too low, it suggests how to guide future action for the greatest profit possibilities.

The booklet is a step-by-step explanation to help you understand what the big concerns call "profit control." They couldn't exist without it, and neither can you. Until you really know your break-even point, for instance, you can't really tell whether your business is in the red or in the black. The 50-page booklet tells you how to prepare your own break-even chart and gives you all the items of cost, both fixed and variable, you'll have to figure into it. It shows you how to analyze profit by several different yardsticks. And of course, like all government books, it ends with a listing of

books, periodicals, and professional and business associations that will help you still further to understand this vital
part of business.

IDEAS ARE WHERE YOU FIND THEM . . .

You must have noticed how other departments besides
the Department of Commerce are getting into the act of
helping you, the businessman. They're doing it right now.
For example: The Department of Health, Education, and
Welfare puts out a directory of *3,660 libraries* which will
lend or rent you literally hundreds of thousands of films
(16-mm) on every subject under the sun. The directory was
put together for teachers, librarians, and community groups;
but what a source of ideas for the businessman! It will cost
you $1.00. Write to the HEW's Office of Education.

Want to get more customers into your store? From this
source alone, you could run a different film every day for two
years without repeating one of them!

The *Federal Handbook for Small Business* is a survey of
small-business programs of various government departments. It's put out by the Senate Select Committee on Small
Business, the House Committee, the White House Committee, and the SBA, all co-operating. You can get it, free, from
the Superintendent of Documents. A run-through of this
book is like opening the door to a treasure vault of business
help. The first chapter covers the SBA. We find a number of
services we have already described in this book and some
we'll take up in later chapters. Business loans, foreign trade
help, buying from the government, and selling to the government are all mentioned. Many SBA publications are sug-
gested for reading.

Going into other government agencies, the *Handbook*

comes up with the idea-sparking suggestions on every page. Let's take a few examples.

1. One branch of the Commerce Department we haven't mentioned up to now is the National Bureau of Standards. Many of this agency's programs benefit small business directly or indirectly. The bureau operates a Building Research Program. If you happen to run a small construction firm without money to spend investigating building materials and structural safety, your government has done it for you. If you have any questions about standards of any kind, a letter to the Bureau of Standards, Washington, D.C., will flood you with information you can count on.

2. If you run a small business and want your employees to have more training, the government will do the job for you. Startling? It's true. The *Handbook* informs us that the Department of Labor will actually train apprentices and other workers in tool and die, printing and publishing, and many other industries.

For additional information on this amazing program, write the Department of Labor, Washington, D.C., for these publications:

Setting Up an Apprenticeship Program
Need a Job
How to Train Workers on the Job
Apprenticeship Training
Apprenticeship Training, a sure way to a Skilled Craft
How to Train Workers on the Job

3. Continuing through the *Handbook,* we find that the Department of the Interior offers topographical maps and information on geological, mineral, and water resources. The Geological Survey has a library of over 100,000 photographs you can buy.

4. The Bureau of Mines (Interior) will keep you informed on health and safety problems of the mineral industry, as well as useful processes for mining, extracting and using minerals, metals, and fuels.

5. Did you know that your government will grubstake you for a prospecting expedition? It's a fact! We quote:

> The Office of Minerals Exploration offers financial assistance to firms and individuals who desire to explore their properties or claims for certain mineral commodities. This help is offered to applicants who ordinarily would not undertake the exploration under present conditions or circumstances at their sole expense and who are unable to obtain funds from commercial sources on reasonable terms.
>
> The Government will contract with an eligible applicant to pay up to one-half of the cost of approved exploration work. The Government's share may not exceed $250,-000 per contract. The operator (applicant) does the work, pays the bills, and submits a monthly report of the work done and costs incurred.
>
> An Office of Minerals Exploration field officer inspects and approves acceptable work, after which the Government reimburses the operator for one-half of the aceptable costs. The operator's time spent on the work and charges for the use of equipment which he owns may be applied toward his share of the cost.
>
> Funds contributed by the Government are repaid by a 5-per cent royalty on production from the property. If nothing is produced, there is no obligation to repay.

If this interests you, get in touch with the Office of Minerals Exploration, Department of the Interior, Washington, D.C., or one of the Department's Regional Offices.

6. Many other bureaus of the Interior offer financial,

research, or other profit-boosting aids in the fields of timber, fisheries, and land management. The National Park Service points out that with the tremendous increase in popularity of the various national parks, more and more opportunities are open for hotels, restaurants, motels, garages, and shops of all kinds to service the crowds, both as concessions inside the parks and on the roads leading to them.

7. Ever dream of the lazy life on a tropic Bali H'ai? The Trust Territory of the Pacific Islands provides loans to locally owned private enterprises. To request further information as to procedures, write to High Commissioner of the Trust Territory of the Pacific Islands, Saipan, Marianas.

The Virgin Islands Government has a tax incentive program to attract industry, including small light industry. For detailed procedures write to Commissioner, Department of Commerce, Government of the Virgin Islands, St. Thomas, Virgin Islands.

The Government of Guam has business tax exemptions for manufacturers and producers. For detailed procedures write to Commissioner, Department of Commerce, Agana, Guam.

The Government of American Samoa has a tax incentive program to attract industry, including small light industry. For detailed procedures write to Governor of American Samoa, Pago Pago, Tutuila, American Samoa.

Well, what more can you ask? Uncle Sam may draw the line at providing you with a golden-skinned beauty for the housekeeping, but short of that . . . it's ask, and ye shall receive!

8. It's not what you make; it's what you keep after taxes that counts. And the Internal Revenue Service wants you to keep every dollar you're legally entitled to. To help the small businessman with his tax problems, the IRS puts out a Mr. Businessman Kit and has other services tailored for you. Still

quoting from the *Handbook,* here's how they describe the service:

> A Mr. Businessman's Kit has been developed for presentation to operators of new businesses as they are formed. Its purpose primarily is to encourage more effective voluntary compliance by helping new businessmen to become fully aware of their responsibilities for filing all the Federal tax returns for which they may be liable, and for paying the taxes due. The Kit is a four-pocket folder designed to hold forms and instructions for preparing most business tax returns. On each pocket is a list of the various forms and documents applicable to the particular business. It also contains a check list of tax returns, a calendar of due dates for filing returns and paying taxes, a convenient place to keep employment tax information for employers, and a pocket for keeping retained copies of tax returns and related materials.
>
> The principal feature of this program, however, is the *personal* presentation of the kit to the taxpayer. Internal Revenue Officers will present the kits and explain the various forms and documents applicable to the particular business. Thus each kit is tailored to the needs of the taxpayer.
>
> The Revenue Officer will make every effort to assist and advise the businessman of his tax filing requirements. A place has been provided on the kit for the Revenue Officer's name, address and telephone number. The businessman will be encouraged to contact the Revenue Officer at any time to obtain further assistance or information.

Tax Guide for Small Business . . .

The Internal Revenue Service publishes annually a *Tax Guide for Small Business* which explains federal tax problems for sole proprietors, partners, partnerships, and corporations.

Income, excise, and employment taxes are explained in nontechnical language, and many examples are used to illustrate the application of the tax laws.

A check list, of particular interest to the new businessman, shows at a glance the taxes for which different kinds of business organizations and business activities may be liable and what the businessman should do about them.

A tax calendar is included, which explains, on a day-by-day basis, what the businessman should do in regard to his federal taxes and when he should do it. The two pages may be removed from the booklet and posted in a prominent place as a reminder of the various tax due dates for the taxes discussed.

Establishing a new business, purchasing a going concern, operating a business, organizing a partnership and corporation, the sale of a business as a unit, the dissolution of a partnership, and the liquidation of a corporation are among the subjects covered in detail in the booklet.

The publication is revised annually to include new rules and changes in tax laws, regulations, and rulings. Plain language is used in the text; supplemented by many examples explaining such things as the need for adequate records and how long they should be retained; employee expense accounts; self-employment tax; declaration of expenses; bad debts; rental expenses and leases; depreciation; educational expenses; how to compute net profit; the cost of goods sold and inventories.

The booklet is available at local Internal Revenue Service offices.

OTHER VEINS TO TAP . . .

If you've stayed with me this far, I hope I've pretty well convinced you of one thing: that you can save time, money, and elbow grease by doing a little reading before you leap into any business plan.

Sounds so simple, you'd think any businessman in his right mind would be doing it automatically. Unfortunately, that's not true. A business executive told me at lunch one day that his organization had spent over $10,000 in travel, research, and high-priced consultation fees to track down a basic fact. "But," he said proudly, "it was money well spent. We plan to base our whole long-range business efforts on this fact."

I'd been collecting and studying government books and pamphlets for years as a hobby and as a necessary tool in my own business (that's how I came to write this book!). My friend's remark nagged at my memory. When I got back to my office I rummaged through my files. You guessed it! I mailed him the little pamphlet he could have bought for a dime, containing all the information he had so expensively and painfully rounded up. He'd never stopped to think that maybe somebody had gone through it all before.

The moral should be self-evident. Never, never, *never* make an important business move without first running a "literature search." This book gives you some idea of the vast resources of the United States Government. However, I'd be shortchanging you if I left you with the impression that Uncle Sam in the *only* rich, generous, and helpful Uncle you have.

Let's make a little detour here and outline some, not all, of the other stockpiles of business information at your command, especially if you live in or near a reasonably large city.

1. State and Municipal Sources

Very much like the federal government, many state, county, and city governments put out reams of printed information. Some of this, being narrower in range and closer to home, may actually be *more* useful to your business than federal information which covers the whole country. You can get state directories on local industrial problems, statistics on car and truck registration, school population, tax collections, maps, employment and unemployment, public health (the possibilities are endless) by writing to the public-relations department in your state capital, county seat, or city hall.

2. Colleges and Universities

Most colleges and universities publish books, periodicals, and other useful material and will furnish title lists on request. The large universities with a school of business administration will have built up stockpiles of business and research information you'll find very valuable. Again, the material is very likely to be gathered close to home, making the information that much more useful to you.

3. Magazines

This time I'm talking about general circulation magazines as well as business magazines. Learn to use the two wonderful reference works you'll find in your public library: the *Readers Guide* (for general magazines) and the *Business Periodical Index* (for business magazines). Articles reaching back as far as twenty years are catalogued by year, title, author, and subject. You are just as likely to find valuable information in a 1947 issue of the *Saturday Evening Post* or *Fortune,* or even the *Ladies' Home Journal,* as you are in *Advanced Management* or the *Zinc Smelters Journal.* Your public library will help you find material on any subject you name.

4. Business and Trade Associations

These range from the National Association of Manufacturers and the Chamber of Commerce of the United States to smaller groups concentrating on a particular business, industry, or area. All of them publish material and are usually glad to give it out to members and nonmembers alike. The publications may be full size magazines like the regularly appearing *Banker* of the American Bankers Association or occasional pamphlets and information sheets. Your local public or university library will probably have some of these in a pamphlet file. Keep your eyes open as you read government publications about your industry: suggestions about private reading material are given quite frequently. Write to the associations direct and they will flood you with material.

5. "Services"

You're familiar with *Dun and Bradstreet, Moody's,* and *Poor's Manuals* in the financial field. Such services abound in great numbers in other fields, too. Examples are *Public Relations News, Real Estate Analyst, Housing Letter.* To locate the service you need, look in the *Handbook of Commercial and Financial and Information Services,* published by the Special Libraries Association, New York City. It lists and describes 577 separate services. Some of these services are expensive to the subscriber, but they're cheap if they lead to bigger profits or help you avoid costly mistakes.

6. Books

I'm firmly convinced that every businessman worthy of the name should have a business library and consult it frequently. My own shelves contain about a thousand books. Maybe you won't want or need that many, but don't be without at least a limited business library. What I'm trying to get across to you is: *don't* try to run your business without taking advantage of the concentrated knowledge, work, and effort of the thousands of people who have gone before you and who have put that knowledge between the covers of books for *you*. That's like driving your car with two cylinders missing.

BIBLIOGRAPHY

Source: U. S. Government Printing Office
Commerce Business Daily $98.80 per year plus $66.90 for Airmail
Official Gazette of the U. S. Patent Office $342.00 per year
U. S. Patents for NASA Available for Licensing 25 cents

Source: General Services Administration Business Centers
Federal Specifications
Government Business Opportunities
Contract Opportunities for Maintenance and Repair of Equipment
Federal Buying Directory
Design for Value—Architect Engineers and Construction Managers

Source: Commerce Dept., National Technical Information Center Springfield, Virginia
Government Inventions for Licensing C51.9/23 $165.00 per year
Weekly Government Abstracts (subjects and prices vary)

Source: The Naval Publications and Forms Center
      5801 Tabor Avenue
      Philadelphia, Pa 19120
Military Specifications and Standards (Army, Navy, Air Force, including MIL and JAN Specifications)

CHAPTER VI

UNCLE SAM AS YOUR
BEST CUSTOMER

SELLING YOUR BIGGEST ACCOUNT
WITH GOVERNMENT HELP

COME ON IN, THE WATER'S FINE!

Have you had the idea that only the industrial giant corporations of this country can do business with the United States Government? Have you felt that you, as a small businessman, didn't have a chance for a federal contract? Well, that's a general feeling among smaller businessmen, and it's absolutely false. The plain fact is that almost any businessman, however small, can have Uncle Sam for a customer, if he really wants to. The government enters into thousands of contracts every year that can easily be handled by small firms. If you're not getting your share of this profitable business, perhaps you should look into it right now.

In most cases small companies shy away from this business because they do not understand the purchasing methods used by the government. They are afraid of the "red tape." So, rather than get bogged down in what they consider complex bidding rules—rather than tackle the paper work—they decide to take a rain check. How wrong they are! Of course there's an amount of paper work involved; of course you have to abide by the rules the government sets down; but once you've taken the trouble to learn the simple procedures required to become one of Uncle Sam's suppliers, almost anyone in your company can handle the details. And when you stop to consider that Uncle can very likely give you *more business* than you're now getting from *all* of your present customers, it's certainly worth the initial effort to get started on this tremendous source of income.

Your "bible" on how to sell to the government is a free book put out by the General Services Administration (Washington 25, D.C.) entitled *Doing Business with the Federal Government.* Reading this book, you'll learn how anxious the government is to cut you in. In framing the Small Business Act, Congress especially directed that small business should receive a fair share of government contracts. The book will give you the how, where, and what of selling to the federal government and will answer most of your questions about the deals you can make.

Once you've read this clearly written, well-illustrated book, a lot of your fears will simply evaporate. You'll be ready to take stock of your own resources and decide what you have to offer that Uncle Sam may need. And he needs plenty! As the country's biggest business firm, the government buys everything from thumbtacks to power plants. This book outlines the basic principles on which the government buys. You're told your responsibilities as a contractor, and you're even given advice on how to buy government owned property. This extremely informative book of some 90 pages is capped off with facsimiles of most of the standard forms you'll need to know about when doing business with your government.

If you can read only one book on this subject, it should be *Doing Business with the Federal Government.* In clear, down-to-earth terms, the first part covers competitive bids, quality control, standards, and specifications the government will insist on. It takes up certain special types of contracts which may be of interest to you. It will also refer you to other publications to keep you informed on changes and new items the government is looking for.

The book covers the various government departments, one by one, and gives you some idea of their needs. A few of these will surprise you. Do you sell small boats, fishing nets, or hiking boots? The Bureau of Commercial Fisheries may be looking for them. Do you make or sell anything that a physician, dentist, or hospital might need? Check into the daily want list of the Department of Health, Education, and Welfare. The Agriculture Library buys books and library supplies. The Maritime Administration is on the lookout for paint, rust preventives, and metal-conditioning compounds. And a real bonanza exists in the Bureau of Public Roads if you can supply road construction equipment and supplies.

All this, of course, only scratches the surface. A much more specific reference work, still from the small business-man's point of view, is the U. S. Government Purchasing and Sales Directory put out by the SBA for $2.35. After a good deal of actual basic information about selling to the government and to government contractors (sub-contracting), it lists in alphabetical order the specific products and services specially needed by both military and civilian purchasing offices. The products range from abrasives to zinc ribbon. There are some 60 pages, covering more than a thousand such products with code numbers following each item to identify the offices desiring that item. Sometimes only one code number follows an item (such as Altar cloths, 506). Sometimes there are twenty or more code numbers, indicating a much wider need for more commonly used items. But following through on Altar cloths (Code 506), for instance, we're in for a surprise. Code No. 506 leads us to all of the

Veterans Administration Hospitals, regional offices, and supply depots—a total of more than a hundred markets for this single item!

And the beauty of it is, you have just as much chance of getting this order as the largest firm in the country. The government only insists on getting quality at a price, exactly like your other customers.

GENERAL SERVICES ADMINISTRATION . . .

While we've concentrated on the Small Business Administration as your particular friend, you don't want to ignore another agency of great value. That's the General Services Administration, which, as the name indicates, is a kind of catchall business and supply agency for the *other* agencies of the government. GSA buys, stores, distributes, and maintains government supplies and property; it also does a lot of the transportation, paper work, and records work for executive agencies.

The Children's Bureau of the Department of Health, Education, and Welfare, for instance, may find it easier and cheaper to get its paper clips, wastebaskets, janitor supplies, or whatever from the GSA than to go out and contract for such things on its own. Since literally hundreds of government agencies do the same, this makes GSA a gigantic and very convenient market for you and the manufacturer or distributor of paper clips, wastebaskets, or janitor supplies. Instead of knocking on the doors of a hundred government departments, you sell a hundred times as much to *one* buyer.

And don't be backward about putting in your oar. The GSA, like the SBA, *wants* to do business with the smaller supplier; you'll be received just as cordially as General Motors when you have something to sell. GSA maintains twelve regional offices throughout the country in addition to the Washington headquarters; so you don't have to travel to do your business face to face. These offices will advise you of the locations of contracting offices; tell you how to get on bidders' mailing lists; where and how to get government specifications so that you'll know your product or service will meet the standards. They'll show you how to keep up to the minute on current bidding opportunities; they'll even give you valuable tips on how to introduce new products to government supply systems and how to promote demand and sales of your present products. In short, they'll knock themselves out to tell you what steps to take, what forms to use, and whom to contact when you want to do business with the government, and all this through trained people whose knowledge is at your disposal at no charge or fee.

Like the Small Business Administration, the General Services Administration puts out heaps of printed material specially tailored for the small businessman looking for a government contract. Some recent books available for the asking are:

Doing Business with the Federal Government
Guide to Specifications and Standards of the Federal Government
Buying Government Surplus Personal Property
Partners in Progress (Minority Business Program)
Federal Buying Directory
Government Business Opportunities
Contract Opportunities for Maintenance and Repair of Equipment

Note that booklet on *Leasing Space to the Government.* The GSA acts as the government's rental agent not only on building and warehouse space but in other fields. For instance: GSA is open for bids on auto-repair contracts and U-Drive rentals at the seventy-five or more motor pools it runs.

Incidentally, you can get a Federal Buying Directory of Washington, D.C., free from the GSA. This is a handy wall-type chart that will help you to identify quickly the various agencies interested in specific products.

One edge the big firm has over the small businessman in competing for government business is know-how. But the GSA does its best to equalize that gap by letting you know exactly what the government expects. A leaflet on *Doing Business with the Federal Government* warns you that you can't simply bid; you've got to merchandise your product just as you would to a private buyer. You've got to satisfy the government that your product or service will do the job economically and efficiently.

It all boils down to one word: *sell.* This goes double when you're introducing a new or improved product or service. The buying official is not going out of his way to sell your product for you; it's up to you to go to the "consumer" —in this case, the agency that's going to use it—and sell *them* on its superiority.

"SELLING TO THE MILITARY" . . .

That's the title of a 90-cent booklet published by the Department of Defense, which is your direct guide and source book in selling to the Army, Navy, Marine Corps, Air Force, and the Joint Agencies.

As you know, the biggest slice of Uncle Sam's budget dollar goes for defense spending, and most of that slice is funneled right back into the business world. Iron and steel, dynamos and transistors, airplanes and ships, are contracted out to private firms to dig, make, ship, and build. Even where the government handles the work on a do-it-yourself basis, salaries and wages are paid to soldiers and sailors, civil-service engineers and steam fitters, planners and draftsmen. What happens to all that money? Why, they spend it to buy the things you sell, of course! So whether your business is apples or zithers, get in there and cash in on the military dollar.

The Department of Defense wants to do business with *all* competent firms; it *wants* competition to be as wide as possible. Small firms and firms in labor surplus areas are especially invited to offer their products to supply defense needs.

That word *needs* is the real key. As in any business, to make a go of it you must learn your customer's needs. Then you must find out his buying policies and follow leads to search out selling opportunities. One of the best ways to find the needs of the government is through the *Commerce Business Daily.*

This is a newspaper published every day (Monday through Friday); subscription is $98.80 a year, plus $66.90 for Airmail. This daily paper keeps you posted on the very latest information you'll need to sell to both the military and civilian sides of the government. All proposed contract awards of over $10,000 are listed, as well as awarded contracts above $25,000. The listing of firms which have received their good-sized contracts is your direct lead for subcontracting opportunities. Most of these firms will want to farm out jobs for parts, subassemblies, services, and supplies to someone, and it might as well be you. To get the *Commerce Business Daily,* make your check or money order payable to U. S. Government Printing Office and mail it to:

Superintendent of Documents
U. S. Government Printing Office
Washington, D. C. 20401

You'll find it one of the best investments you ever made.

WORLD'S BIGGEST CUSTOMER . . .

The military arm of the government uses supplies not only in great quantity but also in bewildering variety. Glancing through the book, *Selling to the Military,* you expect to see calls for ammunition and generators, explosives and jet planes. But golf clubs? Ant farms? Women's panties? Toy soldiers? Caviar? Insecticides? Absolutely! The Post Exchanges and the Quartermaster Corps need just about everything under the sun. The book lists the principal interests of the Military Exchange Service (the Post Exchange or "PX"), which are candy and confections; beverages; tobacco and accessories; toiletries and drugs; stationery and supplies; clothing and accessories; jewelry, toys, housewares, and accessories; sports and recreational equipment and supplies; automotive accessories; food.

Sometime ago, we manufactured plastic toy soldiers to retail at $1.00 for a box of one hundred pieces. Naturally, our primary market was the toy stores in the country. But imagine our surprise when sales to PX's soon began to outstrip our sales to toy stores! And not only did the PX's move thousands and thousands of sets for us, but we had no credit losses, for in effect we were selling to the United States Government.

So the next time you think of selling a product to the government, don't necessarily think in terms of guided missiles or electronic equipment running into millions of dollars; instead, think of our selling these little toy soldiers by the thousands, and perhaps it will give you a broader view on marketing *your* products to Uncle Sam. So jump right in and get your share of the billions of dollars being spent to make our country strong. If you miss out on this fertile source of business, you're not only hurting yourself but passing up a wonderful chance to help your country.

GOT AN INVENTIVE MIND? . . .

How about putting it to work for Uncle Sam? Believe it or not, he'll buy your inventions and pay you good money for them, provided they're what he wants. And he tells you exactly what he needs in *Inventions Wanted,* a free publication of the Department of Commerce. It lists more than six hundred inventions wanted by the armed forces and other government agencies. Just to give you an idea of the scope of inventions needed, here are a few "wants" listed in the book.

> *Self-Luminous Paint.* This paint must be readily seen in the dark, should require no external excitation, emit no harmful radiation, and maintain its brightness for a minimum of five years. Such a paint is required for safe and adequate illumination of instrument dials, meters, signs, etc.
> *Heat-Resistant Paint.* Heat-resistant paint capable of retaining adhesion, film integrity, and color up to temperatures of 1,000°F for extended (2 or more hours) periods of time. *Present situation and requirements:* Paints such as this are available for service only at temperatures less than 650°F.
> *Aircraft Paint.* An aircraft paint which will resist rain erosion at temperatures beyond 300°F at high Mach numbers.
> *New Methods of Making Colored Smokes.* In present smoke mixtures the dye (40 per cent of the mix) is volatil-

ized by an oxidizing material (60 per cent of the mix). About 80 per cent to 90 per cent of the dye is lost by decomposition. A composition or method which would substantially reduce this loss of dye is desired. A possible solution might be the discovery of a mixture of several dye intermediates which can be caused to react to form the dye and at the same time produce sufficient heat to volatilize the dye without undue decomposition.

Self-Luminous Material. Scope: Luminous sheet material which will glow in the dark without external excitation for marking roadways, buildings, obstructions, personnel, etc. If radioactive, the emitted radiation must be below tolerance level. It is essential that the sheet be fabricated from nontoxic materials. Brightness should be minimum of one "effective microlambert."

Sound-Absorbing Material. A lightweight sound-absorbing material for use in helicopters and jet planes that is far superior to present materials. Perhaps it might combine other functions such as armor plate and insulation.

There are few ways in which you can be of more service to your country—and incidentally, benefit yourself—than by applying your inventive talents to these problems.

RESEARCH AND DEVELOPMENT . . .

Research and development is a new and magic word combination. It can be just as important to you, the small businessman, as it is to Rand or Convair. You're invited to contribute your share in this exciting field and to take advantage of the profitable business opportunities it offers.

The Small Business Act of 1958 ordered government agencies to give all possible help to small business in the activities of government research. In the free booklet, *Small Business Guide' to Government Research and Development Opportunities,* you'll find a complete rundown on the contract opportunities open to you. Every department and agency lists its main interests, and you are even told what the individual smaller departments are looking for.

This book contains valuable information on how you can land a big research and/or development contract with the government, and it also refers you to other publications on this subject. You're told how to offer proposals, and any organization or person is free to suggest an idea for research and development. I've been told that amateur cameramen, after studying slow-motion movies made of birds in flight, have come up with the idea of slotted wings for planes—an idea which may revolutionize aviation. As a businessman, you'll think, perhaps, of the type of research connected with your own products. If you are qualified to carry out the research, you'll be favorably considered for the job if the government decides it's worth investigating.

Every business firm interested in getting an R&D contract from the government is asked to prepare a brochure to convince the government that the firm is capable of carrying through the job efficiently and successfully. The valuable booklet we are talking about gives you tips on how to prepare this brochure and what to put in it. Again, remember: this is a *selling job* to convince the technical personnel in the government agency that you can handle the assignment if they award it to you.

Every SBA regional office has a specialist on tap to answer your questions; and there's also a Small Business Specialist at each procuring agency, arsenal, or laboratory who should be contacted first with your ideas. They have your best interests at heart.

Ever think *your* product might land on the moon? It's possible! The National Aeronautics and Space Administration (NASA) is a source of business very much like the military. Send for the free booklet, *Selling to NASA,* which will tell you:

> The supplies and services which NASA buy number in the thousands—from routine office supplies to complex construction projects, from miniature electronic components to large spacecraft systems. Your business, plant or laboratory might well be an important source of supplies or technical know-how in any of a number of important NASA contracts, no matter how small or "routine" your activities may be.

Like the military, NASA wants ideas. It conducts research and development in the same way, looks for the best-qualified organizations, and urges you, if you have an original idea in NASA's field, to submit it without waiting to be asked.

As for products, NASA spends 75 per cent of its funds with private industry and business, along with educational and research organizations. And NASA is going to keep right on spending that way.

It's up to you to get yourself on NASA's bidding list, explaining in detail what you can offer. The purchasing office sends out bidding invitations to the list of suppliers of the items or services it wants. Write to NASA headquarters in Washington, D.C., for the forms you'll have to fill out to get on the list.

For subcontracting, you apply directly to NASA's prime contractors. A Small Business Adviser at NASA headquarters or in any of the centers of NASA activity will give you a list of the prime contractors. He'll also help you in any other way possible. Write to:

> NASA Directory
> NASA Headquarters
> National Aeronautics and Space Administration
> Washington, D. C. 20546

So get started today looking into the opportunities in NASA. The sky's the limit!

BUYING FROM THE GOVERNMENT . . .

When I headed this chapter "Uncle Sam as Your Best Customer," I'm afraid I was holding back on you. Oh, the heading is true; it just doesn't go quite far enough. You see, Uncle Sam wants to sell *to* you as well as buy *from* you. He has a tremendous amount of both land and merchandise, and he offers most of it at bargains you've got to see to believe. So, just as he can be your best customer, he can, in certain cases, be your biggest source of supply at fantastically low prices. Let's look into this big plus right now.

A LAND-OFFICE BUSINESS . . .

That's what the government is running, all the time. Vast areas of land are continually being put up for sale. You may have to get in line behind public agencies—states, civic organizations, and other nonprofit agencies—which are given first refusal and healthy discounts, especially on lands they plan to use for public health, education, recreation, or wildlife conservation. But all other surplus real estate of the government is usually offered for sale through advertising on a competitive-bidding basis.

For a quick run-down on the details and variety of these opportunities, write to General Services Administration for a free leaflet entitled *Disposal of Surplus Real Property*. And to learn of particular sales, with descriptions of the property scheduled to be sold, write the General Services Administration and get your name put on its mailing list for surplus property. These are listed by region, in case you're interested in a particular part of the country.

HOMESTEADS . . .

Homestead land is land the government will give you free if you agree to improve it. A hundred years ago it was possible for a settler to stake out over 500 acres of land, through farming, timber, and grazing tracts. This was the government's way of encouraging our hardy grandfathers to come out and build up the West.

Nowadays, however, there's little agricultural public land left, and the rules have changed. But you can still homestead five acres, sometimes more. If you're lucky you may find a piece you can use for a mountain, desert, or river cabin. You have to build on it within a specified period of time, whereupon it becomes yours. The government charges you nothing, but you may have to pay nominal registering, surveying, and perhaps county charges. Almost all the public domain land left is either in Alaska or west of the Rockies. Much of it is desert or mountain, and all the rest is leased out for grazing, timber, or mining. For information, write to the Department of the Interior, Bureau of Land Management, Washington, D.C.

SMALL TRACTS . . .

Few people know about an attractive opportunity in land through the Small Tract Act of 1938. Any citizen may obtain a tract up to five acres on which to live, play, or establish a business. These lands are not free; some desirable tracts have sold for several thousand dollars. Such expensive tracts may be on a main road or just outside the border of a national park and in a very desirable place to put up a café, motel, or filling station. But it's safe to say that whatever you pay for the tract, it will still be a bargain.

All the information you'll need to put you next to this opportunity can be found in a booklet, *HOW TO BUY PUBLIC LANDS,* available from the Government Printing Office for 25 cents. Instead of buying the tract outright, you may lease it or lease with the right to purchase at a fixed price after two or three years. During that period you must put up improvements (such as a house), as the Bureau of Land Management directs. You can readily see how a tract in a well-chosen location, with the improvements, may be worth much more than the sale price by the time your option is up. Many enterprising businessmen have made a good deal out of this opportunity Uncle Sam offers.

OTHER GOVERNMENT REAL ESTATE . . .

If you're prospecting for minerals, you're welcome to stake a claim in the time-honored way on public domain land, including national forest lands. After complying with the mining laws, you can secure title to the land through a "patent" (meaning "ownership papers," not to be confused with the "invention" kind of patent). Keep in mind, however, that you must have discovered minerals on the claimed spot. If you want to know the procedure for this, obtain

"Suggestions for Prospectors"—40 cents.

If you want to irrigate, cultivate, and improve desert land, you can get it for just a few dollars an acre in the western states. Unfortunately, most of the tracts with the best water sources were grabbed up long ago. You'll have to satisfy the government that you own the water rights and have a plan to irrigate and pay for the land.

Certain deposits of oil, gas, coal, potash, sodium, and phosphates in government lands can be leased or bought. The local land office of the area you're interested in will refer you to the proper source for these deals. In some cases, don't be surprised if you end up doing business with an Indian tribe!

If you are interested in quarrying sand, gravel, or building stone on government lands, you can make arrangements to buy or lease with the Bureau of Land Management or the Forest Service. The same applies to timber and forest products.

Also, grazing rights can be had on federal lands, including the national forests. See the Bureau of Land Management.

And finally, to round out the real-estate picture, you can buy an old fort, a lighthouse, or an island, if such is your wish. General Services Administration inherited real estate to the tune of 9 billion dollars after the end of World War II. Most of this has been disposed of to communities, but there's still a lot of it left. Ask the GSA for listings, which keep changing as more and more of the parcels are put on the market. Many buildings left over from Army camps are still valuable. The GSA sells them usually through sealed bids, but small business gets the edge if the bids are reasonably close. In this type of deal, small business is defined as a concern with fewer than five hundred employees. And you can buy on credit, too. Write to the nearest regional office of the GSA for more information about this.

SURPLUS, IT'S WONDERFUL . . .

Besides real property, the government wants to sell you, at bargain prices, literally mountains of merchandise no longer needed by the agencies which bought it originally. This surplus is not always secondhand merchandise; much of it has never been used. You may find items you can use in your own business, or you may join the many hundreds of traders who buy and sell surplus as a regular business. Since many smaller items are sold in "lots" containing anywhere from a dozen pieces up and since much of the stuff is in its original unopened cases, there's a treasure-hunting element here that appeals to many. Bidding on a lot for a few items in it, you may find something you never realized you bought, which is worth more than you paid for the whole lot.

TO SUM UP . . .

I hope I've convinced you that no matter what your business, it pays you to look into the almost limitless opportunities of doing *some* of your business with Uncle Sam. Through all his agencies for buying and selling, he goes out of his way to favor *you*, the small businessman. You don't have to be big enough to send your salesmen or representatives to the Capital. The government is so eager to buy from you and to sell to you that it practically *comes to you* through the many regional offices of SBA, GSA, and the other agencies.

At the same time, you'll do better for yourself and get the jump on your competition by learning all you can through the books mentioned in this chapter and by making use of the business-service specialists in the government regional offices. Then get your name on the right "bid lists" . . . and good luck!

BIBLIOGRAPHY

Source: General Services Business Service Center

Doing Business with the Federal Government
Guide to Specifications and Standards of the Federal Government
Buying Government Surplus Personal Property
Partners in Progress (Minority Business Program)
Federal Buying Directory
Government Business Opportunities
Contract Opportunities for Maintenance and Repair of Equipment

Source: U. S. Government Printing Office

Selling to the Military, 90 cents
U. S. Government Purchasing and Sales Directory, $2.35
Our Public Lands (153.12) $3.00 a year, single copy 75 cents
How to Buy Public Lands, 25 cents
Selling to Navy Prime Contractors, $1.00
Selling to AEC, 45 cents
How to Do Business with GPO, free

CHAPTER VII

UNCLE SAM AS YOUR BOSS

A Lifetime Job Working
for the Government

I can just hear you screaming.

"*Me,* work for the government? Me, take a job? I'm a *businessman!*"

All right, simmer down. Look at it this way. Suppose I offered you a $100,000 loan, interest-free, put into escrow as your capital investment to go into business. Interested? You can't touch the capital, but suppose I guarantee you 7, 8, or possibly 10 per cent net profit every year on that investment. (You'll have to pay income taxes on it, of course. I'm no magician!)

Not only that, I promise you'll have no payroll to meet, no bills for goods you wonder if you're able to sell, no sales, excise, or social-security taxes to account for, no personnel problems (except yourself), none of those headaches to worry about which you've been reading of in the chapters up to this one—like ratios, advertising, sales territories. Did I mention that you'll work a forty-hour week and will be able to spend evenings and weekends with your family?

But I'm not through yet. Maybe I should have my head examined, but I'll make my offer still more attractive. In case you fail, quit, go bankrupt, or just decide to walk off and leave the business, I'll tear up your I O U, and we're quits.

What is this, a businessman's dream of heaven? Maybe so; but it's also a pretty good description of a government civil-service job. Actually . . .

THERE'S MONEY IN WORKING FOR THE GOVERNMENT! . . .

Not to mention security, sick leave, overtime and vacation time, regular salary increases, opportunity for promotion, valuable training on the job, and generous retirement pay after you've put in your service.

In fact, if you look on government service as a *business,* it stacks up as a pretty darned attractive one. Many a businessman working all hours, worrying himself into ulcers and an early grave, has less to show at the end of the year than the federal employee with the same training, experience, and ability.

What do government jobs pay? It's true that if you are an electronics engineer or an attorney, you can probably make more in private industry or private practice than in government service. The top civil service salary at this moment is around $18,500 per year. On the other hand, if you have merely routine abilities, the government service will pay at least as much as and possibly more than you could get in the employ of an outside firm. The average civil service salary is about $8,000 a year; and that's 8 per cent on a capital of $100,000!

Incidentally, we'll concentrate on civil service in this chapter. There are "excepted" positions, chiefly in the executive branch of the government. They're "excepted" usually because they're of a confidential or policy-level nature. Certain other jobs (such as ambassadorships) are traditionally of a patronage nature; that is, they're appointed without exami-

SCHEDULE OF ANNUAL RATES

GRADE	PER ANNUM RATES AND STEPS									
	1	2	3	4	5	6	7	8	9	10
1	$5,294	$5,470	$5,646	$5,822	$5,998	$6,174	$6,350	$6,526	$6,702	$6,878
	5,017	5,184	5,351	5,518	5,685	5,852	6,019	6,186	6,353	6,520
2	5,996	6,196	6,396	6,596	6,796	6,996	7,196	7,396	7,596	7,798
	5,582	5,871	6,060	6,249	6,438	6,627	6,816	7,005	7,194	7,383
3	6,764	6,989	7,214	7,439	7,664	7,889	8,114	8,339	8,564	8,789
	6,408	6,622	6,836	7,050	7,264	7,478	7,692	7,906	8,120	8,334
4	7,596	7,849	8,102	8,355	8,608	8,861	9,114	9,367	9,620	9,873
	7,198	7,438	7,678	7,918	8,158	8,398	8,638	8,878	9,118	9,358
5	8,500	8,783	9,066	9,349	9,632	9,915	10,198	10,481	10,764	11,047
	8,055	8,323	8,591	8,859	9,127	9,395	9,663	9,931	10,199	10,467
6	9,473	9,789	10,105	10,421	10,737	11,053	11,369	11,685	12,001	12,317
	8,977	9,276	9,575	9,874	10,173	10,472	10,771	11,070	11,369	11,668
7	10,520	10,871	11,222	11,573	11,924	12,275	12,626	12,977	13,328	13,679
	9,969	10,301	10,633	10,965	11,297	11,629	11,961	12,293	12,625	12,957
8	11,640	12,028	12,416	12,804	13,192	13,580	13,968	14,356	14,744	15,132
	11,029	11,397	11,765	12,133	12,501	12,869	13,237	13,695	13,973	14,341
9	12,841	13,269	13,697	14,125	14,553	14,981	15,409	12,337	16,265	16,693
	12,167	12,573	12,979	13,385	13,791	14,197	14,603	15,009	15,415	15,821
10	14,117	14,588	15,059	15,530	16,001	16,472	16,943	17,414	17,885	18,356
	13,379	13,825	14,271	14,717	15,163	15,609	16,055	16,501	16,947	17,393
11	15,481	15,997	16,513	17,029	17,545	18,061	18,577	19,093	19,609	20,125
	14,671	15,160	15,649	16,138	16,627	17,116	17,605	18,094	18,583	19,072
12	18,463	19,078	19,693	20,308	20,923	21,538	22,153	22,768	23,383	23,998
	17,497	18,080	18,663	19,246	19,829	20,412	20,995	21,578	22,161	22,744
13	21,816	22,543	23,270	23,997	24,724	25,451	26,178	26,905	27,632	28,359
	20,677	21,366	22,055	22,744	23,433	24,122	24,811	25,500	26,189	26,878
14	25,581	26,434	27,287	28,140	28,993	29,846	30,699	31,552	32,405	33,258
	24,247	25,055	25,863	26,671	27,479	28,287	29,095	29,903	30,711	31,519
15	29,818	30,812	31,806	32,800	33,794	34,788	35,782	*36,776	*37,770	*38,764
	28,263	29,205	30,147	31,089	32,031	32,973	33,915	34,857	35,799	*36,741
16	34,607	35,761	*36,915	*38,069	*39,223	*40,377	*41,531	*42,635	*43,839	
	32,806	33,899	34,992	*36,085	*37,17	*38,271	*39,364	*40,475	*41,550	
17	*40,062	*41,397	*42,732	*44,067	*45,402					
	*37,976	*39,242	*40,508	*41,774	*43,040					
18	*46,336									
	*43,926									

*The rate of basic pay for employees in these rates will be limited to the rate for level V of the Executive Schedule (as of the effective date of this salary adjustment, $36,000).

nation. And the Armed Services have certain civilian jobs which they fill without civil service procedure.

If you can get one, go to it! But these exceptions aside, you'll have to go through the civil service mill to get your job, whether ditchdigger or federal prosecuting attorney. Your salary will be rated according to a GS number. That means General Schedule. The numbers go from 1 to 18; positions are rated according to difficulty. A GS-3 typist, for instance, will normally be expected to handle more difficult work than a GS-2 typist. Incidentally, to give you an idea of salaries, stenotypists can go as high as GS-7 and earn up to $12,317 per year.

See General Schedule on page 139.

You go up through the grades by promotional examinations, which are held periodically as needed. Furthermore, the government is a big organization, and it covers a big country. You can frequently get transfers into more congenial types of employment or to other localities without leaving your job or endangering your accumulated benefits.

WHAT KIND OF JOB? . . .

Almost all types of occupations found in private industry are also found in the Federal Civil Service. Chances are, whatever your talent, the government has a need for it and is ready to pay you for it. It would be impossible, almost, to list the bewildering variety of civil service positions. Here are a few at random:

Accountant	Business Machine Operator
Apprentice	Carpenter
Athletic Director	Chemist
Attorney	Clerk
Bank Examiner	Correctional Officer
Budget Examiner	Dentist

Draftsman
Economist
Editor
Elevator Operator
Farmer
Forester
Geologist
Guard
Home Economist
Inspector
Insurance Officer
Internal Revenue Agent
Investigator
Jobs Overseas
Laborer
Librarian
Mechanic
Metallurgist

Nurse
Occupational Therapist
Pharmacist
Photographer
Physical Therapist
Physician
Physicist
Post Office Clerk
Printer
Proofreader
Psychologist
Purchasing Agent
Social Worker
Statistician
Student Dietitian
Teacher
Veterinarian
Writer

Note how your business experience could make you a natural for such positions as purchasing agent, bank examiner, or any number of other jobs.

Incidentally, don't hang onto the outmoded idea that the government worker is a shovel-leaner, just putting in the time until he draws his retirement pay. If you get a job with Uncle Sam, not only will you be fully qualified (more about the examinations soon), but you'll put in a full day's work for a day's pay.

Under civil service you have over two million jobs to choose from. Your politics don't count; you don't have to know a congressman or pay a commission to get a position. Visit or write the nearest Civil Service Regional Office and ask to be put on the list for jobs available in your categories. Post offices, as well as most public libraries and public buildings, keep the most recent bulletins posted.

When you're interested in a particular position, read the bulletin carefully. If you don't qualify and no exceptions are indicated, forget that job. The bulletin means exactly what it says, including age limits, height and weight (on some jobs), and particularly education and experience. If you *really* want the job and seem to be missing out by a small detail, get in touch with the Civil Service Regional Office and see if they'll accept your application anyway.

Having applied, you'll be given a written and possibly an oral examination. For some jobs, you may also take a practical test. If you pass, you'll be notified of your position on the eligible list. When your turn comes up, you'll be offered the job. It's true that the employing officer has his pick of the three highest-ranking applicants for the job, and he may not like the way you part your hair. On the other hand, you have the privilege of turning down three offers before you're removed from the list.

HOW ABOUT THAT EXAMINATION? . . .

Take it seriously, but don't be afraid of it. If you qualify for the job you're after, if you know the field, you'll find the written examination tough but fair. Go back to that job bulletin. It tells you *exactly* what will be covered in the examination; no more, no less.

Now, what about the content of the examination? What are the questions like? Obviously, the material will vary from job to job. There will be some basic questions, usually, designed to test your general understanding of the meanings of words, of written paragraphs, of simple mathematics, and the like. The Civil Service Commission puts out a number of pamphlets. In this series, No. 11 gives *Specimen Questions from Civil Service Examinations.* The regional office or the

U.S. Civil Service Commission in Washington will send it to you on request. When you receive it, look over the sample questions. They'll give you an idea of what you'll be up against.

For particular jobs, the questions cover the areas you'd be expected to know in order to hold down the job. To repeat, the examination is nothing to be afraid of if you really qualify for the position and if you've boned up where necessary on the job material, the laws and regulations governing the job, and whatever is described on the bulletin as part of the examination.

THE ORAL INTERVIEW . . .

In all but the most routine positions, a lot of weight is put on the oral interview. Questions will be asked you by a representative of the Civil Service Commission and the supervisor of the department in which you'll work if you get the job. This is nothing more than an employment interview. It, too, is nothing to be afraid of if you know your stuff. The interviewers will assess your personal characteristics, the things they couldn't get from your written test, such as your general appearance and your ability to express yourself and to get along with people. They may give you what looks like a hard time in trying to see how you conduct yourself under fire, how you think on your feet. This interview is generally used for positions in which you'll have to deal with people and in certain higher paid jobs.

PHYSICAL EXAMINATION . . .

If you're applying for a job that requires physical stamina, such as mail-sack handler or forester, you'll be required to take a physical examination which is conducted by a medical officer after you've passed the written test and have had your interview and before you're appointed to the job. The physical examination is, of course, for your own benefit as well as the government's. If you have any doubts about passing it, get yourself checked over by your own physician first.

PLUSES AND MINUSES . . .

Any special skill, ability, or aptitude, such as knowledge of foreign languages, accounting, bookkeeping, or typing, is important in putting you ahead of less qualified competitors on the list. The same goes for education beyond the requirements of the application, particularly if it's education that bears on the job.

Veterans

A veteran gets a decided edge in all government employment. If you had wartime or peacetime military service, you get five free points on your written examination. If you're disabled, it goes up to ten points. Send for Pamphlet 12, *Veteran Preference in Federal Employment,* to learn more about these breaks, which include preference in case of staff reduction, too.

Speaking of handicaps, we quote:

> Each year several thousand persons with serious, permanent physical handicaps take their place in the Government's career civil service through the selective-placement program of the U.S. Civil Service Commission. Since 1942, more than 137,000 disabled workers have joined Uncle Sam's civilian work force.
>
> The Commission-sponsored Governmentwide pro-

gram assures the handicapped of consideration for gainful employment. Yet it operates within the framework of the civil service merit system, providing the disabled equal opportunity for Federal employment but not special preference over other applicants. Not only must the physically handicapped be qualified to do particular jobs, they must also *compete* with nondisabled applicants for such civil service positions. In the light of this requirement, the success of the selective-placement program emphasizes the truth that *properly placed,* the disabled worker is as good as the nondisabled.

Selective placement emphasizes abilities—not disabilities. It is founded on the principle that the physically handicapped person who is placed in the right position is not handicapped on the job. When it certifies a disabled person to an agency for consideration for employment, the Civil Service Commission is expressing its belief that the person is well qualified to do the full job.

On the other side of the ledger, you cannot get a government job unless you are a citizen; but whether native-born or naturalized makes no difference. If you've had a prior criminal conviction, you may be disqualified, or you may be temporarily barred for two years from a civil service job. You'll be fingerprinted if appointed, so it doesn't pay to try to hide such a conviction; however, the government policy is to be quite lenient wherever possible, so don't let a past record keep you from trying for the federal service.

The government demands absolute loyalty of its employees, and the tendency has been to tighten up on Communist, Fascist, or other subversive connections.

You and your wife may both work for the government, but the law forbids appointment of any person if *two* or more members of his immediate family, living under the same roof, are employed by the government. This curious requirement is waived, however, if you're a veteran.

There are other obstacles that can keep you out of the civil service. However, they're the same ones you'd run into in applying for a job anywhere: physical or mental unfitness, false statements on the application, cheating on the examination.

You are *not* required to submit a photograph with your application, and you are never asked about race, color, religion, or political affiliation.

Once you start working for the government, you'll find certain of your rights restricted. You don't have the right to strike, although you can join a union or employees' organization, and there are a number of these, usually divided by crafts, such as the National Federation of Post Office Clerks and the National Association of Letter Carriers.

Your right to engage in political activity is rather sharply curbed. Under the Hatch Act, a federal employee cannot actively work for a political party or candidate; he can vote and sign petitions, and that's just about it.

Incidentally, the general impression is that once he's appointed, it takes dynamite to blast a federal employee out of his job. This is not so. As a matter of fact, I believe it's a little *easier* to fire a government worker who misbehaves than a worker in private employment who is protected by a strong union.

WANT A JOB OVERSEAS? . . .

Uncle has plenty of them: room for a quarter of a million American workers in almost every country in the world. What a chance to see the globe and get paid for it! Again, most of these jobs are civil service, so you get the information in the usual places. In fact, one of the best ways to get an overseas job is to take a job with an agency of the government in the United States. Most overseas jobs are filled by transferred career employees.

DON'T FORGET . . .

Your state, county, and city also employ workers to carry out the functions of their governments. Most of these have civil service setups modeled more or less after the federal system. Sometimes state and local salary lists run higher than the federal pay for the same jobs, too. So, if you want to earn your "profit" on that $100,000 "capital" I offered you at the beginning of this chapter, look into these job opportunities. Most public buildings, courthouses, and libraries keep the current job-opening bulletins on file, or you may write to your state capital, county seat, or city hall for information. Address your letter to the Personnel Board of these agencies.

A FINAL PLUS . . .

Something I've hesitated to mention up to now is the satisfaction of *service.* I realize that most federal workers look on their jobs as routine with the pay check their only goal. But a lot of people are working for the government who could step out and make much more in private industry or private practice. A prime example is the 20,000 or so young people working for the Peace Corps. They make about 11 cents an hour, but they make the sacrifice willingly because they believe they're helping to create a better world. The same applies to top men—scientists, lawyers, businessmen— who could make ten to fifty times their government salaries in the outside world.

In a less idealistic way, I look at the mountains of aid the government heaps on its citizens (you've been reading about a small part of it in this book), and I feel that anyone who contributes to this work deserves our thanks and respect.

BIBLIOGRAPHY

Source: Government Printing Office

Working for the U. S. A., 35 cents
Your Retirement System, 65 cents
The Federal Career Service—At Your Service, 60 cents
The Federal Career Directory, $2.40
Federal Jobs Overseas, 35 cents
A Guide to Federal Career Literature, 45 cents
These Are Yours: Salary, Life Insurance, Opportunity for Promotion, etc. 25 cents
Veterans Readjustment Appointments, 35 cents

CHAPTER VIII

UNCLE SAM AS YOUR PROTECTOR

SAFEGUARDING YOUR BUSINESS
WITH GOVERNMENT HELP

A prominent New York jeweler had a $50,000 diamond and ruby necklace to ship to a customer in Chicago. How did he send it? By special bonded messenger? Not on your life. He wrapped the package in plain brown paper, used his own name and home address for the return address, put on a few stamps, and sent it by *perfectly ordinary parcel post.* He insured it for ten dollars, the way Aunt Mary insures the cookies she sends you for Christmas. And like Aunt Mary's cookies, the package got where it was going. That's Uncle Sam's mail carriers for you. They not only deliver the mail; they deliver it *safely.*

Actually, if your mail gets lost, it's probably your own fault. Address your envelope or parcel correctly and clearly, make sure your return address is also on it, and you can drop it into that familiar red, white, and blue box on the corner and relax. Even with poor addressing, inadequate postage, and badly wrapped packages, the chance of your mail getting lost is less than one in 100,000. You can reduce that chance by keeping mailing lists up to date and by notifying the post office of your own changes of address. You know that even if your customer lives on a country road or fifty miles up the river, Uncle Sam will see—somehow—that he gets the mail you send him.

That's why I say a little prayer of thanks every night for the United States Post Office, and so should you. I don't care what business you're in; you'd have a lot rougher time of it without the mails. Even letters burned in a plane wreck have turned up at my office after going through the hands of the famed "nixie" clerks: those wizards who can make sense out of just about anything.

In my previous book, I said that while the postage stamp is your greatest sales tool, you must bear in mind that it carries a heavy obligation to be scrupulously honest at all times, for Uncle Sam protects the *content* of the mail as well as the mail itself. Through his post-office inspectors, he is working night and day to stop racketeers from stealing your money. As a matter of fact, the inspectors spend more than a quarter of their time running down and halting mail frauds. Besides this, they keep the mails clear of obscene and threatening letters, lotteries, firearms, explosives, and poisons. They're known as such tough lads where criminal statutes are broken that "con" artists will go to great lengths to avoid sending or receiving letters in the course of their crooked business.

A few months back my wife fell for a phony pitch in a newspaper ad. She sent money for a promotional book of "free" neighborhood services, which turned out to be anything but free. I called up the sender and tried to get her money back. He was giving me a hard time, until I casually mentioned that I'd take the matter up with the postal inspectors. I got a check back the next day.

All this is mighty important to you as a businessman. It means that your legitimate business by mail is received with confidence—a confidence backed up by Uncle Sam. He spends millions to keep up the reputation of the mails, and you reap the benefit.

At the same time, it's easy to overstep the rules without really intending to, so I suggest you pick up a *Postal Guide* on your next trip to the post office, read it, and learn the regulations you're expected to follow.

As a businessman, you'll be interested in knowing that when you stamp that letter, you're dealing with the nation's biggest business—actually one of the biggest in the world. The Postmaster-General, the head man in charge of all postal activity, operates 45,000 post offices and employs 600,000 workers with a payroll of $10,500,000 a *day*. He has a fleet of 50,000 government owned cars and trucks and leases another 50,000. Right now, he's going into automation in a big way to help move the mountains of mail you and I and our fellow businessmen pour on him every day.

UNCLE SAVES YOUR MONEY . . .

He saves and protects your money in any number of ways. Let's start with the post office. Although higher interest in other investments has cut into it somewhat, Postal Savings is still the only way thousands of persons save. Their nearest post office is their bank; they accept the low 2 per cent interest rate, knowing that their money is as secure as the government itself.

Probably the most popular direct savings plan offered by the government is, of course, the U.S. Savings Bonds program. E and H bonds are about the safest savings you can find. You buy E bonds at 75 per cent of their maturity value: that is, a $100 bond costs you $75. But if you hold it for the full 7 years 9 months, you can cash it for $100. However, the bond is cashable at any time at any bank. It's value at any period short of maturity is printed right on the bond itself. Your interest is 4¼ per cent for the bond held the full time;

somewhat less if you cash it in earlier. Thus you get a bonus for holding the bond the full period.

The H bonds come in denominations of $500 to $10,000 and mature in 10 years. On these you pay the face value and your interest is 4¼ per cent if held to maturity for the full ten-year period. The interest is paid directly to you by check every six months after the first six months.

Both E and H bonds are universally sold through banks, savings and loan associations, and payroll deduction plans of employers.

Uncle Sam protects your money in other ways than just socking it in his bank. For instance, you don't have to bite every coin to make sure it's genuine. The Secret Service fights counterfeiters around the clock for you and keeps your danger of loss through this crime down to a minimum.

On the other hand, through the Federal Reserve and other agencies, the government preserves the value of your good dollar. It's true that inflation has been eating into it for some time and will probably keep on eating. But the United States dollar is still just about the soundest currency in the world, thanks to Uncle's unceasing efforts to keep it so.

Uncle Sam also protects you when you put your savings into a bank or a savings and loan association. The Federal Deposit Insurance Corporation guarantees your deposit to the tune of $40,000. If you're old enough to remember the time—before 1933—when banks popped like firecrackers all over the land, you will realize the wonderful work this government agency has done in protecting your savings dollar.

In addition, Uncle Sam protects your business dollar through the Federal Trade Commission. This agency stops unfair business practices, interference with normal business competition, and crooked or lying sharpers who prey on other businessmen and the public. Thanks to the FTC, your gold ring marked "14-k" actually contains fourteen-carat gold, and your "100 per cent wool" sweater is exactly that. The FTC stops price-fixing conspiracies and August fur sales that run all year round. The Commission is glad to hear details on possible frauds or misrepresentation. The action they take may not get your money back, but it will clean up the business atmosphere for future dealings. Incidentally, they'll keep your information confidential. The address is Washington 25, D.C.

When you speculate on the stock market or invest your money in stock, as some thirty million Americans do, your funds are protected from sharp practices by the watchful agents of the Securities and Exchange Commission. They keep a file on every new stock and bond issue offered for public sale, making sure that all important facts are available to you in making your choice. The commission watches for abuses that would cheat you of a fair shake in the market; however, it does *not* approve, disapprove, or advise you on any stock or bond issue. Where you risk your money is your own affair, but you have the comfort of knowing that the information on the prospectus is complete and accurate.

Recently, the Federal Reserve Board has set stock margins at 50 per cent. You must put up $5,000 to buy $10,000 in stocks. Margin requirements are changed from time to time, depending on the amount of speculation on credit and the state of the market.

Your freedom to compete fairly with other businesses is protected through federal antitrust laws and is constantly watched over by the Anti-Trust Division of the Department of Justice. Older businessmen will remember the days when business was a jungle in which the big and powerful swallowed up the small and weak. All this was changed by the Clayton and Sherman antitrust laws.

If you're in agriculture, shipping, or the merry-go-round business, to name just a few, you know how your business life depends on the weather. The United States Weather Bureau scientists can't deliver rain or shine, hot or cold weather, to your order (although they're working on it!), but they can do the next best thing by warning you of storms, rain, or fine weather, so you'll know whether to stock ice cream or hot soup in your restaurant, whether to plan on that business trip now or hold off until next week.

People joke about weather forecasts, but farmers trust them. Crop producers have learned that crops grow only during days when the temperature reaches a certain level. By adding "grow" days and subtracting "non-grow" days on the forecast, they save thousands in planning for harvest and shipping.

For daily weather information, your best bet is your local radio, newspaper, or (in some cities) telephone service. The bureau puts out a five-day forecast twice a week. You can also order the *Daily Weather Map* ($16.50 per Year) and the Monthly Weather Review (Commerce Dept. National Oceanographic and Atmospheric Administration, Rockville, Maryland). Free.

UNCLE SAM PROTECTS YOUR PRODUCTS . . .

You don't have to be a farmer to be interested in the safety of meat, milk, or poultry. The Department of Agriculture inspects animals, grades meat and poultry, and keeps a weather eye out to see that processed products, such as sausage and cheese, are not only safe to eat but meet standards so that you get what you pay for and not something inferior or cheaper.

Here's an article I found in today's newspaper.

ANY RESIDUES OF CHLORDANE IN FOOD BANNED
(Washington) (AP). The Food and Drug Administration
announced Monday it proposes to bar from interstate
commerce food crops bearing any residues of the pesticide
chlordane. Tolerances for residues of 0.3 part in a million
of chlordane are now in effect for 47 fruit and vegetable
crops. These were established in 1955, based on 1950 tox-
icity studies.

The Department of Health, Education, and Welfare—
the newest department of the President's Cabinet—has taken
over responsibility for the Pure Food and Drug Laws, as well
as the Public Health Service. Through the efforts of this
department, you can read on the label exactly what any
package contains, plus its correct weight or volume. Dangerous cosmetics, once very common, are now controlled. And
of course the Narcotics Bureau works full time to stamp out
the traffic in habit-forming drugs.

PROTECTION AND MORE PROTECTION . . .

Run down the listings in your phone directory under
"United States Government." You'll be surprised at how
many agencies are protecting your health, your safety, your
children, your old age, your widow.

Beginning with the obvious benefits of protection you
get from the Army, Air Force, Navy, Marine Corps, the FBI,
and the agencies we've already mentioned, the list is long.
The Federal Housing Administration protects your home by
insisting on certain building standards before granting a
mortgage loan. The low down payment and fair terms of
FHA loans has brought home ownership within the reach of
millions who formerly couldn't dream of it.

The Interstate Commerce Commission's Bureau of

Safety and Service is on the job to make rail and highway travel safer for you.

In the air, you're safer because the Civil Aeronautics Bureau is in there pitching to prevent accidents. Every air crash is gone over carefully to discover the cause and to correct matters if humanly possible. One of the earliest CAB cases involved a crash that nobody could figure out until an inspector noticed that a thermos bottle had rolled into the "boot" or floor depression at the base of the joy stick and had jammed the stick. No matter how hard he pulled, the aviator (they didn't call 'em pilots then) couldn't lift the plane out of a fatal dive. The CAB spread the word. Fliers covered the boot in their planes even before a law could be passed requiring it. The CAB authorities can only estimate how many lives were saved through this action alone.

Ever stop to think of the breaks you get from that ogre, the Director of Internal Revenue, because you're a businessman? Maybe you see red at the mention of taxes. Don't let this blind you to the fact that if your income came entirely from wages, you'd be considerably worse off. You'd have no travel, entertainment, or other business expense deductions, no fast depreciation write-off of your plant and equipment, no advantages to gain through leasing your car and other perfectly legal tax savings. Capital gains would be a word rather than money in your pocket; the same goes for the lush 27½ per cent allowances if you happen to be in oil or one of the other "depletion" commodities.

No question about it; as a businessman, you're Uncle's favorite nephew!

GOT ANY IDEAS? . . .

For a new "article, composition of matter, apparatus or process?" If so, run—don't walk—to the United States Patent Office. There you'll join your sixty million or so fellow citizens who every year take out a patent.

We talked in Chapter V about how you might profit by someone else's patent. Here, I'd like to give you a brief run-down on how to protect your own valuable ideas through following a few basic steps.

1. Make sure your idea is practical. Don't waste money and time, as many do, trying to patent inventions that have no earthly use. The Patent Office urges you—and I do, too —to ask yourself first, will people need this? Use it? Pay for it? If the answer is no, forget it.

2. Get witnesses to verify the date you first thought up the idea. If you have a drawing, get a trusted friend to sign and date it. You may not be the only one working on this idea. But if you have the date witnessed, if you keep good records of progress, you may win out in a later dispute. (Incidentally, don't count on a registered letter you mail to yourself. This won't protect you. As a matter of fact, even the witnesses are not *protection,* only evidence. Your invention is fully protected only when it's patented.)

3. Run a search before you plunge. Your idea may not be as new as you think. You can make the search yourself in Washington or at one of the repository libraries in most large cities. Ask your public library to tell you where the nearest one is. However, the Patent Office advises hiring an expert. "The Patent Office prepares an annual list of registered "practitioners," entitled, "Attorneys and Agents Registered to Practice Before the U. S. Patent Office," available from the Government Printing Office.

After you've studied the patents which are close to your own idea, you've got to make up your own mind about going ahead. This is a business decision. If your idea is essentially better than the others, more practical and more saleable, then go ahead. Remember, you cannot cover old features even with a new use. For instance, you can't patent the wheel even if it is a part of your own invention.

Once you decide to go ahead, you'll need an attorney or agent to help you prepare the application. He'll know how to describe your invention, how to push claims for its novelty; he'll know the technical problems and pitfalls. He'll save you a possible rejection. When you get it, the patent is yours for 17 years and may be renewed for another 17 years.

After you obtain your patent, it's up to you to make it a commercial success. For a small fee, the Patent Office will publish a notice on your patent in the *Official Gazette* letting the world know it's available for sale or lease. The Small Business Administration, the guardian angel of the small businessman, will give you lots of helpful advice and information about locating possible buyers and users of your patent.

WANNA WRITE A BOOK? . . .

Just as Uncle Sam protects your invention from theft and misuse with patenting, he'll protect your written material with a copyright. Under the copyright law, a "book" may be anything from a two-line verse to a twenty-volume encyclopedia. It may be anything written, drawn, photographed, printed, or mapped, including movies, musical compositions, lectures, sermons, and speeches, models and designs for works of art.

Unlike getting a patent, which is a long-drawn-out, difficult and expensive job, a copyright can be had without expert help for a few dollars. It gives you the right to publish, sell, reprint, or translate your work into other languages. Anyone who uses your material without your permission is in serious legal trouble.

To get a copyright, wait until your work is in print, then

send two copies of the best edition to the Register of Copyrights, Library of Congress, Washington, D.C. The Register will issue you application blanks on request, free. The book must bear the copyright imprint, "Copyright, 19–, by [author's or publisher's name]." This must be printed on the title page or the page following it. The two copies will be placed in the Library of Congress.

Your copyright will be good for 28 years, and in the final year it may be renewed for another 28 years by yourself or your heirs. It may be renewed only once, however. If you fail to renew, and after the 56 years at any rate, the work falls into the "public domain" and may be used by anyone.

Many writers, among them Mark Twain, have fought long and bitterly against this provision. They argued that after 56 years, even though most books are worthless to their authors anyway, the rare exceptions should continue to benefit the author or his heirs. But Uncle Sam is not likely to relax on this matter.

Although the United States is not a member of the International Copyright Union, we do have agreements with many other countries to respect each other's copyrights. For more information, write to the Register of Copyrights, Washington, D.C.

KODAK, FRIGIDAIRE, COKE . . .

We use these words as part of our language, but actually they are registered trade-marks. If you don't believe it, just try to put out a new camera and call it a Kodak. Eastman Kodak Company will come down on you like a landslide. The firm probably carries the value of that little word on its books at a million dollars.

The history of trade-marks goes way back to the days

when your medieval ancestor knew he could get the best pint of beer at the Sign of the Gilded Boar, or something of the sort. He could turn over a piece of fine china and see the mark of the maker on the back which was the symbol of the maker's pride, reputation, and responsibility for his product.

The government protects your trade-mark from misuse in the same way it protects your inventions and your writings. You register it through the Patent Office. You have to conduct the same kind of search to make sure you're not accidentally stepping on someone else's toes. You can do this yourself at the Patent Office or at one of the repository libraries; and you can probably draw up your own application, which is much simpler than a patent application.

Before you can register it, the trade-mark must have been in use. If you're in a hurry with a new product, just send a free sample to a friend in another state. That makes it "interstate commerce" and meets the law.

The filing fee is $15.00, which you send in with the written application (get this from the Patent Office), a drawing of the mark, and five specimens or facsimiles. The trade-mark when approved will be your property for 20 years and may be renewed for more 20-year service periods as long as it's kept in use.

Your guide for more information is a free booklet, *General Information Concerning Trade-Marks*. For greater detail, obtain a copy of the Code of Federal Regulations, Title 37: "Patents, Trademarks and Copyrights" from the Superintendent of Documents.

YOUR "SECRET"! NEST EGG . . .

I've saved to the end what I think is one of the most remarkable and valuable protections offered to you as a businessman by your government. It's also one of the newest; hence many businessmen either don't know much about it or haven't realized what it could mean to their future.

I'm talking about the recent provision that permits you as an employer or a self employed person to take advantage of social security retirement benefits. It's true! You no longer have to be employed for wages to come under the protective wing of social security. Stop at your nearest Social Security Office, or write to the Superintendent of Documents for *"If You Are Self-Employed"* Your rate as a self employed person is somewhat higher than the rate you deduct from your employee's wages, but it's still a very worth-while thing. Let's take an example at random. If you're 40 now, you only have to contribute for 10 of the 25 years you have to go to reach age 65. Since your maximum earning credit is $7,800 a year, the most you can pay into the fund is approximately $500 per year, or a total of $5,000. At 65 you begin drawing money each month for the rest of your life. If you do not survive to retirement, your widow and dependent children will draw benefits each month to help them overcome the loss of your breadwinning power. Here is one of the best forms of insurance available to the self employed.

Actually, you *don't even have to retire* to get social security benefits but can draw reduced benefits, depending on how much you earn during a particular month. And listen to this: No matter how much you earn in a year, you will still get a *full monthly check* for any month during which your wages are under $100 or (if you're self-employed) you do not "render substantial services" to your company. And if you're over 72, even this restriction is off. You get full payment, regardless of how much work you do or what you earn!

The chances are these figures will be made more liberal as the years go by, too. So if you've had the idea that because you're the boss, you're being passed over and that social security was only for your employees, wake up!

Other booklets that will bring you up-to-date on this valuable protection are listed below in the Bibliography. All are free at the Social Security Office nearest you.

BIBLIOGRAPHY

Copyright, Patent and Trademark

General Information Concerning Trademarks, 50 cents
Patents and Inventions, An Information Aid, 40 cents
U. S. Customs, Trademark Information, 20 cents
Patent Laws, $1.15
Attorneys and Agents Registered to Practice Before the U. S. Patent Office, $3.35

Postal

How to Address Mail, free
Mailing Permits, free
Domestic Postage Rates and Fees, free

Government Printing Office

Postal Service Manual
International Mail
Instructions for Mailers
Directory of Post Offices
Nation ZIP Code Directory

Social Security (GPO)

Your Social Security Handbook, $4.30
Your Social Security, 35 cents
Your Social Security, Retirement, Survivors and Disability, 30 cents
You, the Law and Retirement, 60 cents
If You are Self-Employed, 35 cents
If You Become Disabled, 35 cents
Your Medicare Handbook, 60 cents

Your Social Security Check While Outside the U. S., free
Your Social Security Rights and Responsibilities, free
Where to Write for Birth and Death Records, 25 cents
Where to Write for Marriage Records, 25 cents
Where to Write for Death Records, 25 cents

CHAPTER IX

UNCLE SAM AS YOUR SERVANT AND HOST

LIVING THE GOOD LIFE
WITH GOVERNMENT HELP

CRADLE TO GRAVE . . .

What book has the widest sale in the United States today? Don't look at the best-seller list in your newspaper. You won't find it there.

But you can get it for $1.00 from our old friend, the Superintendent of Documents. It's called *Infant Care,* and it's the most popular government publication ever issued. Since it first came out in 1914 it has been revised more than ten times to keep up with modern developments, based on the wide experience of many doctors, pediatricians, and other experts. Many mothers across the land swear by it; they wouldn't have a baby without it!

At the other end of the rainbow of life, you can send another 80 cents for *Planning for Later Years.* This one discusses part-time work, activities for your suddenly expanded free time, where to live after you retire, how to make your retirement income stretch; and it also gives you some idea of the community services open to the older person.

Between these two extremes are thousands upon thousands of government publications aimed at helping you—not only "you" the businessman whom we've been looking at so far in this book, but you, the person: the consumer, vacationer, student, hobbyist, eater, drinker, entertainer, shopper, traveler—these are all the different "yous" outside of your business life, and our government has something for all of them. In this chapter we'll throw in a grab bag of odds and ends. Just because they're not directly related to business, don't turn off your business antenna as you read about them. *Everything* is grist to the smart businessman's mill, if he keeps his eyes open. Remember the chapter on ideas; ideas are where you find them, and it could just as easily be in a pamphlet designed to tell the housewife the best way of preserving tomatoes or how to buy a new freezer.

HELP FOR THE CONSUMER . . .

While campaigning for election, the late President Kennedy announced: "The consumer is the only man in our economy without a high-powered lobbyist in Washington. I intend to be that lobbyist."

When he was elected, the President was as good as his word. In a message to Congress he said, "Consumers, by definition, include us all. They are the largest economic group in the economy, affecting and affected by almost every public and private economic decision. Two-thirds of all spending in the economy is by consumers."

He went on to describe some of the consumer's needs: to be protected from false labeling, packaging, and other sharp practices in marketing; safer transportation, food and drug protection, meat and poultry regulation, financial protection from mail frauds and exorbitant credit and interest charges, control of housing costs and quality. He stressed the

UNCLE SAM AS YOUR SERVANT AND HOST

need for consumer information and research as well as consumer representation in government.

This last is of special interest to us because it's what this book is about. The President said, "Too little has been done to make available to consumers the results of pertinent Government research." He ordered the creation of a Consumers' Advisory Council; also, he directed every federal agency to designate a special assistant to work on this problem; and finally, he asked the Postmaster-General to display sample government publications in the post offices and make it easier for people to buy them.

The speech is a landmark in consumer protection. You can get a copy of it from your congressman. Ask for Document No. 364 of the 87th Congress, Second Session. The program that the President outlined there had only a short time to get under way before his death. It remains to be seen whether the program is pushed ahead now or allowed to drag its feet.

UNCLE SETS A GOOD TABLE . . .

But right now, what has Uncle Sam to offer you, the consumer? Quite a bit. The Department of Agriculture alone has published more than 3,000 nontechnical booklets, most of them free, for the farmer, the housewife, the do-it-yourselfer, and just about everyone who shells out his money for food, clothing, shelter, and entertainment. Booklets tell you how to raise vegetables in the back yard, how to repair the roof, and when to spank the baby. Write to the Office of Information, U. S. Department of Agriculture, Washington, D. C. 20250, for a free copy of List 5, for current publications and prices. Here are a few of the titles listed:

UNCLE SAM AS YOUR SERVANT AND HOST   167

Family Fare, 95 cents
Nutritive Value of Foods, 85 cents
Clothing Repairs, 60 cents
Fix Clothes to Make Them Last Longer, 30 cents
Food Guide for Older Folks, 40 cents
Helping Families Manage Their Finances, 95 cents
How to Prevent and Remove Mildew, 25 cents
Removing Stains from Fabrics, 40 cents
Simplified Clothing Construction, 50 cents
Food and Your Weight, $1.00

Incidentally, you can get up to ten of the pamphlets free, in spite of the listed prices.

An Agriculture Department book you'll find extremely readable and useful—or at least your wife will—is the current hardbound *"Food and Nutrition,"* an Agriculture Yearbook. It is crammed with basic recipes, menus, guides, tables of nutrition values, and many money-saving suggestions. You can get it for $7.85 from the Superintendent of Documents.

While we're on agriculture, this department maintains a Special Consumer Assistant, as do most of the other departments. You can reach this official at the home office of the department, 14th Street and Independence Avenue, S.W., Washington 25, D.C. He will answer any questions you have, or he'll refer you to someone who can. Also, the Department of Agriculture runs an Institute of Home Economics. Most of the titles we've mentioned come from it. The institute is constantly experimenting and reporting on new and improved cooking methods and has a healthy interest in the housewife's budget dollar.

This department offers many services not so well known to the average citizen, and some of them are particularly interesting to the businessman. For instance, the Foreign

Agricultural Service concentrates on developing foreign markets for agricultural products. It is constantly sifting marketing opportunities and aiding suppliers and others in the food industry to use them.

The Forest Service has charge of the National Forest lands, which, believe it or not, add up to about one-third of the total land area of the nation. The government is interested in seeing that our forests are not ruthlessly destroyed and goes in heavily for conservation, tree planting, and control.

The Agricultural Marketing Service does marketing research and deals in surplus food commodities. It administers the National School Lunch program which provides a midday meal and milk for millions of needy school children.

And finally, just hitting the high lights, this very important department maintains the largest government library next to the Library of Congress. You're welcome to use any of its 1,200,000 volumes on all fields of agriculture, through loans, photocopying, reference, and bibliographies. Just send the Library a query about the field you're interested in.

UNCLE TAKES YOUR TEMPERATURE . . .

If you work with epoxy resins, the government will supply a pamphlet advising you how to avoid the skin troubles such chemicals sometimes cause. That's just a sample of how Uncle Sam is concerned—and in what detail!—with keeping you alive, healthy, and contented.

Not many of us work with epoxy resins, but more common ailments are around; and the government takes notice of them. You can get a booklet on *Watch Your Blood Pressure,* for instance. When the President proclaimed April, 1963, as Cancer Control Month, the Superintendent of Documents made a special effort to acquaint the nation with the literature he had on this grim killer. Here are some of the publications featured at that time:

Cancer of the Colon and Rectum, 25 cents
Treating Cancer, 45 cents
Progress Against Leukemia, 30 cents
Cancer of the Skin, 30 cents
Cancer of the Stomach, 25 cents
Cancer of the Mouth, 25 cents
Hodgkin's Disease, 25 cents
Danger, Cancer Quacks, 30 cents

And for a general run-down of health and medicine, you can order the *Medical and Health Related Sciences Thesaurus.* This book of 213 pages contains over 12,000 medical and health terms.

HE KEEPS YOU WELL . . .

The late President Kennedy's well-publicized interest in physical fitness resulted in a flood of printed material on the subject and saw the creation of a President's Council on Physical Fitness. Three of the best-illustrated booklets this council put out are:

Adult Physical Fitness, 85 cents
Youth Physical Fitness, $1.30
The Fitness Challenge in Later Years, 75 cents

HE SAVES YOUR LIFE . . .

One of the most valuable books you can own will cost you only one dollar. Write to the Superintendent of Documents for a copy of *Survival, Search and Rescue.* This Air

Force Manual is included with the survival kit of every U.S. military airman and tells you how to get along, take care of yourself, and eventually get back in one piece under all kinds of conditions.

You don't have to be a military airman to profit by this book. Any camper, fisherman, boatman, hiker—any outdoorsman of any description—may find himself in a position where a single line from this invaluable book can mean the difference between life and death. The book is filled with illustrations, showing pictures of edible and poisonous plants, for instance, or exactly how to make an Arab-type headdress to protect you from wind or sun in the desert. The purpose of the book is to aid and insure your survival and rescue regardless of geographic location or climatic condition. The manual tells you what to do, and when, where, and how to do it, whether your survival situation be in the Arctic, desert, or tropics, on land, sea, or ice.

THE BABY DEPARTMENT . . .

The Department of Health, Education, and Welfare is the "baby department" in more ways than one. It's the newest addition to the President's Cabinet, having been created only in 1953. Its very existence is proof of the new government interest in the welfare of the consumer because, as the name implies, it is devoted to our health and our children's education and, besides, is a catchall for a number of agencies whose purpose can only be grouped under the general name of "welfare." Some agencies, such as the Public Health Service, were transferred here from other departments. This agency includes the office of the Surgeon-General and a Bureau of Medical Services (which is responsible, among other duties, for keeping the United States free of dangerous communicable diseases); it co-operates with the states in preventing, controlling, and treating disease and the elimination of hazards to health. It is not generally known that the National Library of Medicine holds the greatest collection of medical literature in the world, with over a million entries on its card index. Thousands of journals in a hundred languages are computer-coded so that a researcher can find out what has been accomplished anywhere in the world in any medical field.

READING, WRITING, AND NUCLEAR PHYSICS . . .

If you (or members of your family) are interested in vocational education, the Office of Education probably has a grant or scholarship waiting for you (or him, or her). The same thing applies to persons preparing to enter (or who have entered) the fields of "agriculture, the distributive occupations, home economics, trade and industry, practical nursing, and the fishing industry." I put quotes around that because otherwise you wouldn't believe how broad the scope is. And this is only a small sampling of the grants, scholarships, and other aids open to help young people train for occupations which the nation feels will be useful.

I've mentioned before in this book that a dollar saved is equal to the profit on ten to twenty dollars of sales. If a supplier offered you an item for a dollar less than you formerly paid, you'd grab it, wouldn't you? That is, if the quality was the same. Well, the quality of education you get on government grant is identical with the kind you shell out $250 to $2,500 per year for—at the same schools and colleges, and under the same teachers.

So, if any member of your family is going to school or plans to go, send to the Office of Education, Department of

Health, Education, and Welfare, 330 Independence Avenue, S.W., Washington, D.C., for a list of the grants and scholarships, with requirements and applications, that may be offered in any particular field of study.

For instance, under the Fulbright Act thousands of Americans study abroad each year or do teaching or research in foreign countries. There are other special fellowships for Latin America, Finland; and there's financial aid for undergraduate students and summer students abroad.

The National Science Foundation, Atomic Energy Commission, and Public Health Service also offer help to students, trainees, and research scholars. And don't forget the giant work of the G.I. Education and Training Program. About ten million veterans have taken advantage of G.I. schooling to complete their education and to get special training in many fields.

YOUR BOOKSTORE! . . .

The Library of Congress will see that any serious student gets any book or other materials in its vast collection. The Library has over 30 million items on file, including maps, photographs, phonograph records, sheet music—anything that can be printed. Through modern microfilm and photoduplication methods, you can get the benefit of whatever you need without taking the trip to Washington.

SOCIAL SECURITY . . .

The really important agency of HEW (Health, Education, and Welfare), as far as you—a businessman and consumer—are concerned, is the gigantic and growing Social Security Administration. If you draw a pay check, you are familiar with the famous "deducts," one of which is for your Old-Age and Survivor's Insurance. We talked about this in Chapter VIII as it applied to the self-employed person. If you're employed, the provisions are the same, except that the payment is shared by your employer and doesn't cost you as much.

Whether you work for yourself or for a boss, it will pay you to study your rights and benefits under this program. Go to your nearest Social Security Office and pick up *Your Social Security*. This tells you how you earn them, how much credit you need to get the benefits, how to estimate the amount of benefit you'll be getting when you retire, and at what age.

The "survivor" part of social security means that the widow or widower of a social-security beneficiary also gets support in the form of a lump sum at the death of the breadwinner and monthly payments for widow and minor children.

IF YOU BECOME DISABLED . . .

This is the title of another social security booklet you should look into. You can get a copy at the nearest Social Security Office. It tells you how long you must have worked under social security to get benefits, how seriously disabled you must be, and how to make your application.

Some other social security pamphlets you can get free are:

Your Social Security
Your Social Security, Retirement, Survivors and Disability
If You are Self-Employed
If You Become Disabled
Your Social Security Rights and Responsibilities
Your Social Security Check While Outside the U. S.

KIDDIE DEPARTMENT . . .

The Children's Bureau was transferred to Health, Education, and Welfare when this new department was created. It doesn't provide direct care of children, but many a mother has raised a child on the pamphlet *Infant Care* we spoke about earlier. About eight and a half million copies of this little manual have been distributed, and I'd guess that one child in three in this nation has benefited from it. The Children's Bureau publishes other valuable pamphlets and books, some popular, some technical. Here are a few of the most useful titles:

> *Infant Care*
> *Prenatal Care*
> *Your Child from one to six*
> *Your Child from Six to Twelve*
> *The Adolescent in Your Family*
> *Your Gifted Child*
> *Your Children and Their Gangs*
> *Older Children Need Love, Too*
> *A Creative Life for Your Child*
> *Child Advocacy*
> *A Situational Approach to Delinquency*

There are seventeen additional pamphlets on *Facts and Facets of Delinquency,* and the bureau puts out a bimonthly magazine, *Children.* You can get copies of all these for the asking. Apply to the Children's Bureau at the local or Washington address of HEW.

And these are not dry-as-dust government type pamphlets, either. In the joyous spirit which seems to infect all who work with and around children, even the staid old Government Printing Office gets into the act! An example is a series called *Headliners.* One of these is a *Pogo Primer for*

Parents (TV Division), in which Walt Kelly's delightful car-
toon characters advise parents on how to handle the problem
of television watching in relation to children. It warns parents against letting the TV set "watch the children," takes up
the matter of violence and frightening elements, and concludes: "Do not wind your child up and set him to watch the
TV set unguided. Do not wind the TV set up and set it to
watch the child. A machine is bad as a sole companion. It
needs help. You can help it. Love your child."

HOME, SWEET HOME . . .

There was a time when you had to save up in advance
and produce 50 per cent or more as a down payment to buy
a house. Or you floated the first 50 per cent with a ruinous
second—and sometimes third—mortgage. Mortgages were
written with a gigantic "balloon" payment at the end which
hung over your head until the last cent was paid. Your home
could be snatched away from you. Naturally, under these
conditions, home ownership was a "sometime thing," and
then only for the upper crust of the financial pie.

Later, largely due to federal education of bankers and
others, it was realized that a man would lose his shirt before
he'd risk losing his home—that the home owner was the
safest risk on record. Bankers loosened up. Then came the
Federal Housing Authority, willing to lend up to 97 per cent
on a housing loan. No more second and third mortgages, no
more balloon payments. Result: You and I and the man who
hauls the garbage can own a home, too! Actually, the FHA
does not lend the money; it merely insures the bank or lending organization against the loans they make to home owners. In so doing, however, the FHA calls the shots, keeping
interest low and down-payment figures to a reasonable

amount, and—what is probably just as important—insists on high standards in housing construction and conditions.

Here are some of the books you can pick up at lending institutions or FHA offices or can write for to the Office of Public Information, Federal Housing Administration, Washington 25, D.C.

> *Selecting and Financing a Home,* 30 cents
> *Buying and Financing a Mobile Home* HUD, Free
> *Get the Facts Before Buying Land* HUD, Free
> *A Guide for Vets Planning to Buy or Build Homes with GI Loans* HUD, Free

For a complete run-down on what Uncle Sam can offer you to make your home cheaper, safer, healthier, and happier, write to the Superintendent of Documents for PL 72, *Homes.*

BE MY GUEST! . . .

Uncle Sam maintains hundreds of vacation spots for you to enjoy. As an American citizen, you're part owner of the hundreds of millions of acres of mountain, forest, desert, and seashore lands comprising the National Park and National Forest systems. Two hundred national parks await your pleasure, each one offering its own individual attractions, from the bears and geysers of Yellowstone to the mysterious swampland of the Everglades. You have the Grand Canyon, Bryce Canyon, Mt. Rainier and its glaciers, Crater Lake, the Grand Tetons in the West and Abraham Lincoln's birthplace, the Cumberland Gap, the Edison Laboratory in West Orange, New Jersey, and hundreds of other historical and scenic spots in the East. They cover our country; there's bound to be one or more near you. The list is a fascinating treasure house of infinite variety. You have Uncle's word that these jewels will never be overrun with high-rise apartments, disfigured by billboards, or priced out of the reach of your pocketbook. The government controls food and lodging prices and provides informed and courteous rangers to help you have fun, whether your idea of fun is fishing, hiking, swimming, driving, camping, or just plain loafing. No hunting and no guns are allowed within national-park borders; and this is the reason the numerous animals and birds are so tame and unafraid.

As an old national park vacationer, I can't urge you strongly enough to try out Uncle's hospitality if you've never done so. Send to the National Park Service, Department of the Interior, for two booklets describing all the parks and monuments in the system. One covers the eastern United States, the other the West. You'll be briefed on the extent of the open season, the facilities, exhibits, accommodations (which range from camping and tourist cabins to luxury hotels like the Ahwanee in Yosemite), the activities, guided trips, and other information you'll want.

During your stay, you'll be treated like a king—or should I say landlord? You'll get a breath of fresh air, and nature in its most beautiful state will spread before you; you'll come home refreshed and renewed.

Do I sound a little wild? I've been accused of conducting a love affair with the Government Printing Office; let's say the National Park Service is my second light o' love, and that won't be far wrong!

THE WELCOME MAT'S OUT FOR YOU . . .

For an entirely different kind of vacation, still with Uncle as host, try visiting him at home. Plan a visit to

Washington, D.C. There are few more exciting spots in the nation than its capital, the center and focus of all the department activity we've been talking about. Before you go, send for two pamphlets to get acquainted with what you'll see in this city of magnificence, beauty, and history. *Know Your Capital City* (25 cents) and *Our Capitol* (30 cents) are fascinating to read, even if you never get to go to Washington. The first tells all about Washington's colorful history and gives you the descriptions and information on the famous landmarks and government buildings. The second book details the story of the Capitol Building. You learn how and when it was originally built and how it grew to its present form. All the history and tradition of its paintings, murals, statues, and furnishings is told. Both books are illustrated.

You'll also want the *U.S. Government Manual* ($5.75) to make your Washington visit more complete. This official organizational handbook of 761 pages and illustrations tells all about every department, bureau, and agency of our government: where it is, who operates it, what it does. It's a valuable reference book you'll find useful in many ways.

Here, too, you are reminded at every turn that *you* own the place. Most of the public buildings are open for touring, from the White House and the Capitol to the big GPO itself.

HOBBY LOBBY . . .

Perhaps you feel that this chapter has wandered away from the original theme of our book, which is "business." Not at all; for keep in mind that you're more than just a businessman; you're a whole man (or woman), and outside interests are just as important to keeping you going in business as, well, eating. Sir William Osler, the famous physician, said, "No man is really happy or safe without a hobby, and it makes precious little difference what the outside interest may be—botany, beetles or butterflies; roses, tulips or irises; fishing, mountaineering, or antiques—anything will do so long as he straddles a hobby and rides it hard."

Hobbies can *directly* influence and help your business, too. A talent for golf has put many a man farther ahead than his business ability warranted.

Collect stamps? Given a big boost by F.D.R., who was a stamp collector of the first water, the Philatelic Agency of the Post Office Department takes in a nice clear profit of up to 5 or 6 million dollars a year from stamps that will never travel on an envelope. These, of course, are picked up by people who make stamp collecting their hobby. The government knows that collectors will flock to the post office for blocks and sheets of every new commemorative issue that comes out, and so plenty are issued. The nice thing about collecting uncanceled United States stamps is supposed to be that you can almost always get your money out if you change your mind about keeping them. Don't count on this. Certainly you won't get it from the post office. They won't take back stamps, for sanitary reasons. You'll have to find a company to buy them from you for commercial use, and you'll have to offer a hefty discount. With more and more big companies using precanceled mail, that market is shrinking. The only alternative is to send out a heck of a lot of Christmas cards yourself!

Profit from stamps? Sure, if you know your stamps. There's a superstition going round that if you had bought a sheet of every issue put out from the time you were old enough to reach the post-office counter, you'd have a fortune in stamps today because of the rarity value. This, unfortunately, is not true. Some issues have advanced on the collecting market; but stamps are put out in such mountainous quantity that very few of them have a chance to become rare within your lifetime.

However, don't let that stop you from collecting or

teaching the youngster to collect. There's no more fascinating and educational hobby open to the person of modest income. Read up on the subject, learn the angles, and you'll have your fun and profit, too.

Coins are a different matter. They're always good for face value and inevitably go up at least a little with the years because, as time goes by, fewer and fewer remain in proof, mint, or fine condition. The mint sells proof sets each year; a set consisting of a cent, nickel, dime, quarter, and half-dollar may be ordered from the Superintendent of the Mint, Philadelphia 30, Pennsylvania. Any coin dealer will show you how to preserve the beautiful satin finish of the coins by mounting them in plastic. And you can watch them grow slowly but surely in value over the years.

Like stamps, coins are more fun if you know all about them. Read up on the subject. A good beginning is two free publications you can get from the Bureau of the Mint, Washington 25, D.C., called *Know your Money* and *Our American Coins.*

AND OTHERS . . .

Stamp and coin collecting are just two popular hobbies that come to mind immediately. But without looking the matter up, I'm willing to venture that you couldn't take up a hobby in which the government doesn't offer you some help. To step up the status scale, I have a handsome book put out by the Smithsonian Institution, *Automobiles and Motorcycles.* It contains 150-odd slick-paper pages of description and illustrations, many in color, of the museum's collection of classic automobiles and cycles, dating back to 1869! This collection includes the Duryea car, thought to be the first American automobile driven by an internal combustion engine. Names like Haynes, Apperson, Daimler, stud the magnificent collection described here. If a serious car collector were asked to choose one car he could take out and own, he'd without doubt go for the Simplex Speed chain-drive. It represents all that is grand in the cars of the brassbound era, a truly mighty engine and beautiful clean lines. Only a few of these cars remain intact today, and the Smithsonian has the best of them.

This booklet is National Museum Bulletin No. 213 and may be had free from the National Museum, Washington, D.C.

WANT TO SPEAK A FOREIGN LANGUAGE?

How about French, German, or Spanish? Many basic language courses are offered by the Superintendent of Documents. They range anywhere from $2.00 to $7.50 per set, and even tape recordings can be purchased to supplement these excellent textbooks.

TO SUM UP . . .

Since hobbies are as numerous as people, I won't try to go into more detail here. All I need say is, if you've kept reading up to this point, you should be pretty well convinced, as I am, that whatever your interest, from archery to zoology, from coin collecting to foreign languages, you can get help, information, instruction, and encouragement from our government's vast storehouse.

BIBLIOGRAPHY

Source: Superintendent of Documents, Washington, D.C. 20402
   Infant Care, $1.00
   Planning for Later Years, 80 cents

Food and Nutrition (Agric. Yearbook), $7.85
Adult Physical Fitness
Youth Physical Fitness
Prenatal Care, $1.05
Your Child from one to Six, $1.05
Your Child from Six to Twelve, $1.15
The Adolescent in Your Family, 55 cents
Your Gifted Child, 55 cents
Your Children and Their Gangs

Family Fare, 95 cents
Nutritive Value of Foods, 85 cents
Composition of Foods, $2.85
A Guide to Budgeting for the Family, 25 cents
A Guide to Budgeting for the Retired Couple, 25 cents
Clothing Repairs, 60 cents
Fix Clothes to Make them Last Longer, 30 cents
Food Guide for Older Folks, 40 cents
Helping Families Manage Their Finances, 95 cents
How to Prevent and Remove Mildew, 25 cents
Removing Stains from Fabrics, 40 cents
Simplified Clothing Construction, 50 cents

Food for Fitness, 25 cents
Food and Your Weight, 40 cents
Calories and Your Weight, $1.00

Home Canning of Fruits and Vegetables, 35 cents
Home Freezing of Fruits and Vegetables, 55 cents

Catalog of Guides to Outdoor Recreation, $1.05
Selecting and Financing a Home, 30 cents
Source: Housing and Urban Development
Buying and Financing a Mobile Home
Get Facts Before Buying Lands

The Capitol, $1.50
U. S. Government Manual, $5.75
A Guide to Historic Places of the American Revolution,
    $1.90

Back Country Travel in the National Park System, 70
    cents
Boating Regulations in the National Park System, 40 cents
Camping in the National Park System, 50 cents
Fishing in the National Park System, 40 cents
Winter Activities in the National Park System, 50 cents

Room to Roam, $1.20
A Catalog of Outdoor Recreation Guides and Facilities,
    $1.05

Practical Spanish for Border Patrol, $1.25
French Units 1–12, $3.00
French Units 13–24, $3.45
French Supplementary Units 1–15, $6.15

CHAPTER X

UNCLE SAM'S BARGAIN STORE

A Treasure of Information
with Government Publications

OPEN SESAME!

When Aladdin first set foot inside the treasure cave, he didn't stop to make a catalogue of the goodies it contained. He didn't classify the pearls for size and luster, the gold for fineness, the diamonds for carat weight. He didn't have to, because he realized he'd stepped into something the like of which the world had never seen, and it all was his for the taking.

Well, this is somewhat the feeling I got when I first heard about the Government Printing Office, and it's a feeling I hope you've shared by reading this book. Actually, you have to visit the GPO to realize its gigantic scope and sheer size. It's an eight-story building with over 32 acres of floor space where giant high-speed presses turn out over 140,-000,000 books and pamphlets each year. Besides the mail business, there's a real bookstore where you can browse around yourself, examing the literature available. The Government has been in the printing and binding business since before the birth of our Republic. Initially, both were necessary for maintenance of public records. But for 75 years, the

Government Printing Office has served the public in another equally important way, by distributing pamphlets, books and booklets, and other materials of interest and value to millions of Americans. All seek to enhance and enlighten our lives and to furnish knowledge of concern to scholars and researchers.

Under the direction of the Public Printer, the Assistant Public Printer (Superintendent of Documents) is responsible for the sale of certain government publications produced by the Government Printing Office.

This sale is largely a mail-order business and involves receipt each day of an average of 25,000 letters and approximately 2,000 telephone calls. More than 20,000 different government publications are stocked for sale. Millions of orders are received annually for many more millions of publications which embrace such diversified subjects as farming, child care, aviation, cooking, homemaking, construction, health, housing, education, ecology, atomic energy, mining, engineering, reclamation, waterpower, American history, weather, interstate commerce, census, business, foreign trade, immigration, finance, transportation, wildlife, laws, political science, labor, national parks, forestry, Army, Navy, and Air Force publications, space, radio, and international relations. In 1921, with the rapid growth of information bureaus and headquarters of various national organizations in Washington, local demand for government publications necessitated the establishment of a retail bookstore on the first floor of the Government Printing Office, known as the MAIN BOOKSTORE. In this largest of Documents Department Bookstores, approximately 2,200 titles are displayed in 2,300 square feet of space. Visitors are able to browse without being crowded, despite the fact that more than 100,000 customers a year are served.

Frequently, the Government Printing Office is invited

to exhibit and display United States Government publications at seminars, library workshops, trade shows, and national conventions. Despite the yearly increase in the interest shown in United States Government publications, our contacts with the public indicate that a large percentage of the population is still unaware of the diversified selection of publications available for purchase from their government.

An innovation of the late '60's was the expansion of the government bookstore concept inaugurated in Washington, which now includes five other Washington-area bookstores, in addition to the main store in the Government Printing Office, and out-of-town stores located in Chicago, Kansas City, San Francisco, Boston, Los Angeles, Atlanta, Dallas, Denver, New York, Pueblo, Canton, Birmingham, Detroit, Philadelphia, Cleveland, Seattle, Milwaukee, and Jacksonville.

And incidentally, as a businessman, you'll be happy to learn that the GPO runs at a profit. While trying to price the books as near cost as possible, the office, every year, turns back to the United States Treasury a surplus of around $5,000,000 left over after expenses and rebuilding stocks are satisfied.

THE LAST ROUNDUP . . .

You can see from the size of the GPO store that, like Aladdin, I couldn't begin to classify and bring to you in this book one hundreth part of their offerings. In the preceding chapters I've only tried to whet your appetite so you could find out more for yourself. Weekly, the mailman brings me lists of new items put out by the various departments and agencies. If I waited for the last of them, this book would never see print; so a halt has to be called somewhere. How-

ever, I can't drop the matter without giving you a final
glimpse of the fantastic variety of the publications that pour
out of the GPO. So, without apology, here's one last free-for-
all, hodge-podge bag of books. Not all of them will be of
interest to you, of course. But you'll surely find something
in the bunch to make you sit up and read! So, grab your hat
. . . hold on . . . and let's go!

Let's start with "the top twenty-five"—the twenty-five
best sellers at the GPO, which by their continuous response
have shown that they fill real needs of the people. We've
already told you about a few of them, but there's nothing
here that won't bear a little repetition.

1. *Food and Nutrition, Yearbook of Agriculture.* This
yearbook on food contains simple basic recipes, menus,
food guides, tables of nutritive value and calories. What to
eat for better health and greater energy, how to gain or
lose weight, how to stretch your food dollar, how to plan
and cook meals your family needs and enjoys, which foods
babies, children, teenagers and adults need, and much
more. $7.85.

2. *Family Fare.* Packed with facts about foods and
cooking—nutrition guides, food plans, buying and storage
hints, menu aids, and many tasty recipes—this useful
pamphlet has been prepared specially for the homemaker.
It includes a complete index of these recipes, a list of
cooking terms, suggestions on ways to use leftovers, and
a list of ingredients that can be substituted for those not
immediately on hand. 90 cents.

3. *Nutritive Value of Foods.* Presents three tables on
the food values in about 500 foods commonly used in this
country, the yield of cooked meat per pound of raw meat,
and recommended daily dietary allowances. 85 cents.

4. *Food and Your Weight.* The calorie values in common foods, a table of the desirable weights for men and

women, and brief discussion of the body's daily calorie need and some basic weight-control facts. In addition, it includes suggestions for reducers and for those who want to gain weight and helpful ideas for planning a day's food. 40 cents.

5. *Wood Handbook.* Designed as an aid to better and more efficient use of wood, this volume covers the structure of wood, physical properties of wood, grades and sizes of lumber, gluing of wood, plywood and other cross-banded products, control of moisture and shrinkage of wood, painting and finishing of wood, fire resistance of wood construction, wood preservation, heat insulation, and many other informative facts about wood. $7.95.

6. *Removing Stains from Fabrics, Home Methods.* Provides up-to-date information on removing stains from various types of fabrics, including stain removal suggestions for the newer man-made fibers and those with special finishes. It describes the proper use of the four types of stain removers—absorbent material, detergents, solvents, and bleaches—and other chemical stain removers. Specific directions for removing all kinds of individual stains. 40 cents.

7. *Starting and Managing A Small Business of Your Own.* Describes the common problems of launching small business operations in general, suggesting specific steps to help those interested in starting and managing a small business to arrive at sound decisions concerning these problems.

8. *Manual of Traffic Control Devices.* Widely accepted and time-tested traffic control practices in the design and application of control devices, as well as extensive research into the principles of safe and orderly movement of vehicles and pedestrians. It includes specific standards for expressway signing, a major section on signing and marking for contracting and maintenance operations, and a brief treatment of civil-defense signing. $3.50.

9. *Our Flag.* Unfolding many historical facts about

our flag, this booklet relates the story of the Stars and Stripes; brief notes on various early American flags; instructions on displaying the flag; and approved flag customs. 70 cents.

10. *Your Social Security.* Describing your social security rights and responsibilities, this booklet provides details on retirement, survivors, and disability payments; amount of work required; events that stop payments; kinds of work covered; procedure for checking your account; and other helpful information. 35 cents.

11. *Infant Care.* The most popular government publication ever issued, this book revised ten times since it first appeared in 1914, provides the information needed by parents in caring for their baby, especially a first baby. Based on the experience of many doctors, pediatricians, nurses, child-development and other experts, it is designed to help parents understand many phases of infant care, such as feeding, clothing, care, growth and development of the baby. $1.00.

12. *Your Baby's First Year.* This short picture leaflet on the care of a baby for his first year of life is designed for quick reading and covers the most important points in good baby care. In its 32 pages it discusses briefly the baby's needs, such as foods, vitamins, sleep, love, play, and clothes; his growth and development; signs of sickness; and other points of similar interest. 50 cents.

13. *Effective Revenue Writing 1.* A basic course designed to give a brief, practical review of writing principles, grammar, and punctuation, this volume presents grammar in a practical way by showing the functions of words or how they may be used. It covers sentence sense, naming words, agreement and reference, tense of verbs and verbals, mood and voice, modifiers, connectives, punctuation and good sentences, word relationships, the effective sentence, and a writer's guide to current usage of some words and phrases. $2.15.

14. *Effective Revenue Writing 2.* An advanced course

designed to help experienced writers and reviewers diag-
nose and cure writing weaknesses. It discusses the nature
and function of written communication, the significant
diagnosing of sentence deficiencies, the role of grammar in
writing, the semantic problem, putting words to work, the
syntax of strong sentences, economy in writing, using
modifiers effectively, parallelism, linkage, logic and syntax, and style in expository writing. $1.75.

   15. *Federal Benefits for Veterans and Dependents.*
This fact sheet is designed to provide *only* general information concerning most federal benefits enacted by the
Congress of the United States for veterans, their dependents, and their beneficiaries. It discusses benefits for veterans of the Spanish-American War, World Wars I and II,
Korean conflict, peacetime veterans, six-month enlistees,
and for those in active service. 60 cents.

USE REVERSE ENGLISH . . .

   Before going on, I want to caution you once more, as I
have done throughout this book, to look at the references
with a broad and, if I may use the word, creative eye. There's
every likelihood you'll get out of them something that even
the writer or the bureau which put them out never thought
of.

   Let me give you an example. The Department of
agriculture has a publication called the *Insects, Agricultural
Yearbook.* This comes from the Plant Pest Control Division
and is basically designed to help farmers, industrial en-
tomologists, and "other agricultural workers," as the foreword clearly states. I don't suppose the creators of this important but highly specialized bit of literature had any other
views of its usefulness when they described a decrease in
citrus mites in Florida and an increase in green peach aphids

in Arizona. Certainly, they never expected it to be avidly
read by a city boy who wouldn't know which end of a hoe
was which.

Nevertheless, I read it regularly. Why? Because, as
I've mentioned before, one of our best-selling mail-order
items is a fly killer called Fly Cake. From this periodical,
describing the activities of insects in various parts of the
country, we learn where the housefly is increasing, and
we concentrate our advertising in those areas to get maximum effect. So you see, it *is* possible to make a silk
purse out of a sow's ear; all you need is a little imagination!

WATCH THE BIRDIE . . .

A photography magazine had some mighty nice words
to say about the series of books the Air Force and the Navy
have put out to train photographers. They're not primers,
but textbooks. Each chapter has quizzes and problems to
help you keep up with the material. To an eager camera bug
who wants to learn more about his hobby, these books are
pure gold. Here they are:

Method for Determining Resolving Power of Photo-
graphic Lenses C13.4:533, $3.25
Photographers Mate 3 and 2, $9.00
Photographers Mate 1 and C, $5.15
Electric Current Abroad, 85 cents
Basic Electricity, $4.55
Basic Electronics V. 1, $5.15
Basic Electronics V. 2, $3.20

A FEW MORE HOBBYHORSES . . .

Raising Rabbits. Nice pets; good stew, too! 30 cents.
Hamster Raising. Not for eating, but they can be both fun and a business. 25 cents.
Weather Forecasting. You, too, can be cussed out by your friends when you make a mistake!
Ducks at a distance. A must for sportsmen, students, bird watchers, this book colorfully portrays the waterfowl in the attitudes you'll most commonly see them take. It tells you what to look for in identifying shapes, colors, voices, flight patterns, rising views, and flock formations. 50 cents.
Backpacking in the National Forest Wilderness. Written for those city folk who dream of exploring the vast wilds but don't quite know how. It tells how to choose equipment, gives sample menus, lists organizations where you can get more information. And it lists by states the wilderness-type areas of the national forests for you to choose from. 40 cents.
Attracting Birds. Tells you how to bring the beautiful feathered folk to your home, how to feed, water, and protect them, and how to see that you don't overdo it, since there are hazards (for man and the birds) in too great a concentration. 25 cents.
Recreational Boating Guide. Takes up the growing sport of boating. You get federal laws, guidelines for safe and enjoyable cruising, even what to do in an emergency. $1.30 And while we're on the water:
Skipper's Course. Designed for crew members of the U.S. Transportation Corps, but just as valuable to the private boatman or boat owner. You'll read about small-boat and shiphandling, piloting, weather, regulations, $1.50.

SHOCKING NEWS . . .

Starting at my own level of knowledge about electricity, electronics, radar, and radio—which is rock bottom—you can learn *How to Keep Electricity from Killing You* (35 cents) in a humorously illustrated booklet put out originally for Navy personnel. From there on you can go into the stratosphere and beyond, with titles like:

Electrical Fundamentals (Alternating Currents) $3.05
Electrical Fundamentals (Direct Current) $2.65
Troubleshooting and Repair of Radio Equipment, $4.40
Basic Electricity, $4.55

NO LONGER FOR LOVERS . . .

The nations of the world are casting a cold eye on the moon with an idea of dividing it up into real estate. Our own country, never backward in enterprise, is ready to sell you—believe it or not—*Charts of the Moon!* That's right, dear reader! The Air Force has charted the moon in extremely fine detail at a scale of one inch to 16 miles and sells it off in sections (charts, that is) 22 by 29 inches each, and in color. You can order your charts at $5.50 per subscription, pick out your vacation spot, and head for it by the next rocket!

Meanwhile, before you blast off, you can watch out underfoot for *Poisonous Snakes of the World* ($6.90), put out to save Navy personnel, wherever they might be, from the most dangerous species of serpents. It has numerous colored photographs of the most typical and common species.

Going down nature's path, you can get books on:

Grass. Devoted to grassland agriculture, this year book discusses the needs and uses of the more common grasses and legumes as well as the place of grasses, legumes, and associated plants in animal feeding, conservation, crop rotation, farm management, soil building, and other related fields. (Cloth) $9.00.

Trees. Tells how and why to plant trees and care for them; explains the essentials of choosing, planting, and growing trees as a farm crop, as a renewable natural treasure, and as a necessary part of city and country life. It has chapters on specific problems or values: insects, fire, recreation, wildlife, forestry, and economic importance. (Cloth) $9.10.

Water. Presents a series of articles by outstanding authorities on a subject that is of interest to everyone. Among the many topics covered are: water and soil conservation; irrigation; industry's need for water; water pollution; weather cycles; floods; water and wildlife; safe water supplies; and water laws. (Cloth) $8.10.

Soil. In 800 fact-filled pages, 142 leading authorities tell you what you want to know about such subjects as soil structures and types; fertilizers; organic matter; compost, mulches; economies of moisture; soil management in your region; soil management for gardens, lawns, flowers, vegetables; and many more. (Cloth) $8.25.

Land. Gives a wealth of information about our vast public domain; the increasing size of farms and our declining farm population; government programs; Indian lands; land in Alaska and Hawaii, our two new states, and Puerto Rico; land in subdivisions; highways; tenure; irrigation; forests; and a host of other related subjects. (Cloth) $7.60.

Seeds. In well-written informative chapters, this unique book presents the complete story of seeds: why seeds are important to you; how seeds develop, travel, rest, grow, and carry life onward; how men produce, improve, clean, store, test, certify, and sell seeds of all kinds; what modern science has learned about the effect on seed production of various factors; what all buyers of seeds should know about seed laws, frauds, good and poor seeds, weeds, costs. (Cloth) $7.10.

And to wrap all this up, there's:

After a Hundred Years. What does the agricultural revolution of this century mean? How does it affect me? This Centennial Yearbook answers these questions in 108 chapters and hundreds of pictures. It is a treasure of information about outstanding developments in farm practices, scientific methods, plants, conservation, forests, animals, insects, machines, food, clothing, markets, trade, books, homes, and problems we all face. It is a book about people. It is for everyone who wants a better understanding of our changing world, for everyone who loves the country. (Cloth) $8.05.

PLANNING YOUR FUTURE WITH GOVERNMENT HELP

Choosing a career? Changing jobs? Counseling others about these decisions? The facts are at your fingertips in a 792-page reference book on nearly seven hundred occupations and thirty major industries. This reference book is called *Occupational Outlook Handbook* and sells for $6.85 from the Superintendent of Documents, Government Printing Office, Washington, D.C. 20402.

If you are only interested in a particular field, you can buy any one of dozens of reports from accountants, advertising, or architects to railroads, restaurants, or television and radio broadcasting. These occupational outlook reports range in price from five cents each to fifteen cents each and can really help you to decide on what career to follow. These reports are invaluable to parents, students, teachers, employees; etc.

A LOOK AT HISTORY . . .

The United States has a long and glorious history, and Uncle Sam wants all his nephews and nieces to know as much about it as possible. So that you can own the basic documents of our nation, he offers you a set of facsimile reproductions of the Nation's Charters of Freedom. The Constitution, the Bill of Rights, and the Declaration of Independence are now available on three pages suitable for framing. These three facsimiles, prepared from the parchments on display in the National Archives at Washington, D.C., faithfully reproduce the yellowish tint and faded brown ink of the originals. The four sheets of the Constitution have been reduced and reproduced on one large page. The Bill of Rights and the Declaration of Independence are about the same size as the original documents. Copies of these freedom documents should also be a worth-while addition to every American home. The individual documents are priced:

> The Bill of Rights (facsimile). 33 by 31 inches. 90 cents.
> The Constitution of the United States (facsimile). 38 by 31 inches. 90 cents.
> The Declaration of Independence (facsimile). 36 by 29 inches. 90 cents.

Going ahead in our history, you can follow the pioneers step by step through thirty-six fascinating booklets covering events and describing historical places. The titles in this Historical Handbook Series are:

> *Custer Battlefield* (Montana). The story of General Custer and the battlefield where he made his "last stand."

Jamestown (Virginia). The first permanent English settlement in America.

The Lincoln Museum and the House Where Lincoln Died (District of Columbia). Portrays the story and scene of the assassination of Abraham Lincoln.

Saratoga (New York). The defeat of the British forces at Saratoga may be considered to mark the turning point of the American Revolution.

Fort McHenry (Maryland). Gives the events of history surrounding the birth of our National Anthem.

Custis-Lee Mansion, The Robert E. Lee Memorial (Virginia). The history of the home of Robert E. Lee.

Morristown (New Jersey). The story of two critical winters of the Revolutionary War.

Hopewell Village (Pennsylvania). Tells about the establishment of the early American iron industry.

Gettysburg (Pennsylvania). Relates the history, campaign, and Battle of Gettysburg. The story of the establishment and dedication of the cemetery and the events leading to the famous "Gettysburg Address" delivered by Lincoln.

Shiloh (Tennessee). Scene of the first major engagement in the western campaign of the War Between the States, this handbook describes the preliminary campaign and the first two days' battles on April 6 and 7, 1862, and gives the results of the battle at Shiloh.

Statue of Liberty (New York). Gives the story of one of the most symbolic structures in the United States.

Fort Sumter (South Carolina). Describes in detail the construction of Fort Sumter, the events leading to the firing of the "first shot" of the Civil War, and the Federal bombardments of the fort from 1863 to 1865.

Petersburg (Virginia). Tells of the fighting which centered around Petersburg, the scene of decisive military operations that cut the Confederate lines of communications between Richmond and the South and led to the capture of the Confederate capital.

Yorktown (Virginia). Describes one of the most momentous events in American history.

Manassas (Bull Run) (Virginia). Presents the history of two of the more famous battles of the Civil War, the First Battle of Manassas, July 21, 1861, and the Second Battle of Manassas, fought approximately a year later, which paved the way for Lee's first invasion of the North.

Fort Raleigh (North Carolina). Tells the story of the Lost Colony.

Independence (Pennsylvania). Describes Independence Hall and the signing of the Declaration of Independence.

Fort Pulaski (Georgia). The age-old struggle between offense and defense is the principal story of Fort Pulaski. Giving numerous details about the construction of the fort, this pamphlet also reveals many dramatic events which led to its siege and surrender.

Fort Necessity (Pennsylvania). Describes the action at Fort Necessity during the French and Indian War in colonial America.

Fort Laramie (Wyoming). A story of the Indian Wars in the West.

Vicksburg (Mississippi). Gives the history of the campaign and siege at Vicksburg, the last Confederate stronghold on the Mississippi River, in June, 1863.

King's Mountain (South Carolina). The southern campaign of the American Revolution.

Bandelier (New Mexico). Preserves the ruined dwellings of the most extensive prehistoric Indian populations of the historical Southwest.

Ocmulgee (Georgia). Describes one of the first large Indian sites in the South to be scientifically excavated.

Chicamauga and Chattanooga Battlefields (Georgia-Tennessee). Relates the Battle of Chickamauga and the struggle for control of Chattanooga, the gateway through the mountains to the heart of the Confederacy.

George Washington Birthplace (Virginia). The story of the Washington family plantation in Westmoreland County, Virginia.

Montezuma Castle (Arizona). Describes the pueblo ruins in the Verde River Valley of central Arizona.

Scotts Bluff (Nebraska). Tells the story of this celebrated landmark on the great North Platte Valley trunk line of "the Oregon Trail."

Chalmete (Louisiana). Site of the Battle of New Orleans, the last big battle and the greatest American land victory of the War of 1812.

Guilford Courthouse (North Carolina). Describes a battle which marked the beginning of the end of the Revolutionary struggle.

Antietam (Maryland). Described in this pamphlet are the interesting events leading to the violent conflict of two great armies, colliding almost by chance, which shattered the quiet of Maryland's countryside on September 18, 1862—the bloodiest day of the Civil War.

Vanderbilt Mansion National Historic Site (New York). Presents the history of the Vanderbilt Mansion and the Vanderbilt family, with a detailed, illustrated description of the mansion and its grounds.

Richmond Battlefields (Virginia). Briefly describes some of the events and battles that took place in the vicinity of the Confederate capital.

Wright Brothers National Memorial (North Carolina). Tells the story of Wilbur and Orville Wright and their successful flight at Kitty Hawk and gives a brief description of the points of interest at the Memorial.

Fort Union National Monument (New Mexico). This pamphlet, well illustrated with pictures, photographs, drawings, and maps, relates the story of the founding of Fort Union in 1851, the part the fort played as guardian of the Santa Fe Trail, and its participation in the Apache War, the Ute War, the Civil War, and other campaigns, until its abandonment in 1891.

    Aztec Ruins National Monument (New Mexico). This historical handbook tells the story of the men in the San Juan Valley—early hunters and gatherers, the Basketmakers, the Pueblos, and the Aztec Pueblo. It describes the exploration and excavations of these well-preserved ruins, as well as the ruins as they are today.

    And for more recent history, you can refer to a new edition of the *Public Papers of John F. Kennedy.* Here you'll read verbatim transcripts of the President's speeches, news conferences, messages to Congress, and other materials. The book is the latest edition in a series of Papers of the Presidents of the United States.

    And history is not restricted to words, either. For $2.50 you can order a set of fourteen full-color reproductions depicting heroic exploits of American fighting men. These are reproductions of paintings hanging in the Pentagon—paintings that graphically depict scenes of heroism and courage by American fighting men in every war in which this nation has been involved, from the American Revolution to the action in Korea. They provide an inspiring gallery of art that vividly reminds us why America has remained a free nation since we declared our independence 200 years ago. Each picture contains a brief description of the action portrayed. Titles are:

    Merry Christmas, 1776. Trenton, New Jersey, December 26, 1776. At dawn General Washington's artillery opened a surprise attack at Trenton. This victory over superior forces was a turning point in the war.

    The Road to Fallen Timbers. Ohio, August 20, 1794. Tracking down the Indians of the Northwest who had twice whipped our Army, the Legion met with the foe on the banks of the Maumee, Ohio, routed him from behind a vast windfall, and destroyed his warriors.

"Those Are Regulars, By God!" Chippewa, Upper Canada, July 5, 1814. As the American troops advanced steadily through murderous grapeshot, the British commander opposing them realized his mistake in believing them to be the untrained levies he had easily whipped before. In this battle at Chippewa, Upper Canada, this crack brigade of United States infantry drove the British from the battlefield.

"Remember Your Regiment." Resaca de la Palma, Texas, May 9, 1846. In an attack that climaxed the opening campaign of the Mexican War, a squadron of the Second Dragoons slashed through the enemy lines.

First at Vicksburg. Confederate Lines, Vicksburg, Mississippi, May 19, 1863. The First Battalion of the Thirteenth Infantry lost 43 per cent of its men in this bitter battle during which the soldiers of both sides demonstrated their bravery in hand-to-hand combat.

Good Marksmanship and Guts. Near Fort Kearney, Wyoming, August 2, 1867. Thirty men of the Ninth Infantry chose to stand and fight when attacked by some 2,000 Sioux Indians in the Wagon Box Fight near Fort Kearney. Suffering only three casualties in the fight, this small force killed and wounded several hundred Sioux.

Gatlings to the Assault. San Juan Hill, Santiago de Cuba, July 1, 1898. During the assault on San Juan Hill in the war with Spain, the Gatling Gun Detachment gave fire support to the attacking infantry. This, the U.S. Army's first use of close-support machine guns in the attack, was decisive in the capture of San Juan Hill.

"I'll Try Sir!" Boxer Rebellion, 1900. During the fiercely opposed relief expedition to Peking in the Boxer Rebellion, when two companies of the U.S. Army's Fourteenth Infantry Regiment were pinned down by heavy fire between abutments of the Chinese City Wall, a trumpeter

from E Company volunteered to make the first perilous ascent of the wall.

Knocking Out the Moros. Philippines, June, 1913. In the four-day battle of Bagsak Mountain on Jolo Island, Americans of the Eighth Infantry and the Philippine Scouts brought to an end years of bitter struggle against the fierce Moro pirates.

"The Rock of the Marne." Near Mezy, France, July, 1918. In their first taste of combat, the Thirtieth and Thirty-eighth Infantry Regiments of the Third Division kept the crack troops of the German Army out of Paris in the historic Battle of the Marne.

Raid on Ploesti. May 31, 1944. B-24's of the Fifteenth Air Force attacking the refineries at Ploesti, an important source of petroleum products for the Nazi war machine. These raids on strategic Nazi industries curtailed production and forced the Nazi government into a costly program of industrial maintenance, reconstruction, and rebuilding underground.

"Follow Me!" Leyte, October 20, 1944. In the face of heavy machine-gun and rifle fire from Japanese pillboxes on Red Beach, the leading elements of the Third Battalion, Thirty-fourth Infantry, U.S. Army, were led forward by the Regimental Commander and succeeded in establishing a beachhead on Leyte.

Remagen Bridgehead. March 7, 1945. Although the Ludendorff Bridge crossing the Rhine at Remagen was mined for demolition and its destruction was imminent, the men of the Ninth Armored Division rushed across the structure without hesitation and seized the surrounding high ground. This, the first bridgehead across Germany's formidable river barrier, contributed decisively to the defeat of the enemy.

Breakthrough at Chipyong-Ni. Korea, February, 1951. When the men of the Twenty-third Infantry were cut off from the Eighth Army and surrounded by Chinese

Reds, an armored unit smashed through to save the trapped soldiers and their arms.

More than a million of these fine paintings have been sold since the government first put them on the market.

MORE HISTORY . . .

For $4.50 you can get the *Guide to Federal Archives Relating to the Civil War*, describing government records during the 1860's: 721 pages of solid, documented statements on the most interesting and bloody conflict of our history.

Or turn to *Image of America*, an illustrated catalogue of photographs taken from the early days of the art through the turn of the century, depicting various aspects of American life, history, and progress to about 1900. The catalogue contains 46 reproductions and describes more than 300 other photographs in various categories.

MAPS . . .

Did you know you can get an aerial view of your own home so clear that you can count the lilac bushes in the front yard? The Department of Agriculture supplies aerial photographs of any section of the United States (restricted areas excluded, of course) at $2.10 for one 18 by 22 inches or $5.50 for 40 by 40 inches. The large print is scaled at 400 feet to the inch. If you want a map of a western section, send to Western Laboratory, Performance Division, Commodity Stabilization Service, Department of Agriculture, 2505 Parlays Way, Salt Lake City 9, Utah. For an eastern map, send to Washington 25, D.C., as usual.

The Department of the Interior Geological Survey also

offers topographic maps of any section of the country. These come in a number of scales and at various prices. Send to the Geological Survey, Washington 25, D.C., for more detailed description.

And if you feel like becoming a do-it-yourself-mapper, you can learn how through *Photogrammetric Mapping,* an engineering manual giving all the principles and procedures. Cost, 40 cents.

To help you with this stimulating hobby, you might go for a wall chart on the Metric System, for 50 cents, giving units and definitions, conversion tables, and even a recent change to a wave length standard of length, as well as a section on temperature scales.

And before we leave the subject of maps, how would you like to know something about them? You can learn all about it through *Elements of Map Projection* ($2.75). This 220-page illustrated book tells you in simple language and diagram about the ideas behind map and chart construction. By the time you've gone through it, you'll not only have a more complete understanding of what it takes to make a map and a greater respect for the men who make them; you'll be able to construct a map yourself.

CHOW'S ON! . . .

Agriculture and HEW, through their consumer and home-economic services, publish many books on cooking—so many that I won't begin to try to list them here. One sample is *Family Fare,* mentioned at the beginning of this chapter among the "top twenty-five" government best sellers. Another is *Tips on Cooking Fish and Shellfish.* But you ought to know that Uncle Sam has experience in feeding his nephews not individually, but by the thousands, in the

Armed Forces. And the series of Navy Recipe Service cards, listing taste-tempting recipes covering many varieties of dishes, should be ideally useful for institutions serving large groups. The cards come with index separators, ready to file.

A FINAL WORD . . .

Well, there it is. Obviously, I could go on and on. Books on art, books on music . . . did you know that the Navy publishes a *Hymnal* and a book on music theory?

You can win many a bet by convincing your open-mouthed friends that they can't name a subject, from A to Z, from the cradle to the grave, from athlete's foot to space travel, on which Uncle Sam hasn't published some useful information!

How can any American survey this treasure-trove without feeling a surge of love and pride, without voicing a silent prayer of humble thanks for the privilege of being part of a nation truly "of the people, by the people, and for the people."

CHAPTER XI

A BASIC GUIDE TO EXPORTING

I. GETTING STARTED

How can a firm that knows nothing about exporting or international trade find a foreign market for its products? This booklet is designed to show you that it can be done, that exporting is neither mysterious nor difficult. It contains the basic steps and information to enable you to begin the exporting process. U.S. companies ready to exploit the opportunities in exporting will find there is substantial help available, both from Government and private sources.

Where should you begin? As a preliminary step you should first assess your export potential.

ASSESSING EXPORT POTENTIAL

Because exporting does require an extension of a firm's resources, an assessment of your export potential is just good business. Briefly, this assessment should consider: Industry trends, your firm's domestic position in the industry, effect exporting may have on operations, status of your resources, and the anticipated export potential of your products.

This basic information will give you a good picture of your firm's capablities and the export potential of your products—necessary information you will need before expanding into exporting.

RESEARCHING FOREIGN MARKETS

The next step is to locate foreign markets where products such as yours are in demand. There are many sources of such information, both Government and private.

Government Sources

One of the best sources of such information is the Bureau of Census' monthly *Foreign Trade Report FT 410 U.S. Exports Commodity by Country*. The *FT 410* provides a statistical record of the shipments of all merchandise from the United States to foreign countries, including both the quantity and dollar value of these exports to each country during the month covered by the report. Additionally, it contains cumulative export statistics from the first of the calendar year. From this you can learn which of more than 160 countries have bought any of more than 3,000 U.S. products. By checking the *FT 410* over a period of 3 or 4 years you can determine which countries have been the largest and most consistent markets for products like yours. These reports are available singularly or on a subscription basis and are on file at Department of Commerce district offices (see page 50) and at many public or university libraries.

Another Commerce publication, *Market Share Reports*, gives a statistical picture of international trade in manufactured products, covering more than three-quarters of the total exported output of all the free world's factories.

The publication shows trends in the movement of goods between countries over a period of several years. It includes data on imports of more than 1,100 commodities by more than 90 countries and reflects both changing levels of import demand in those countries and shifts in the relative competitive positions of exporting countries. U.S. shares of the market for more than 1,000 selected commodities in major markets are given in percentage terms.

Market Share Reports enable the business executive to compare his firm's export performance to any specific market during the years covered with that of his industry as a whole or with that of manufacturers of the same product in other countries.

The Commerce Department also can supply you with extensive foreign economic data including such factors as population by age, income, literacy levels, ownership of appliances and automobiles, industries and types of manufacture. Also available is information on such topics as trade and tariff regulations, quotas, licenses and exchange permits.

The Bureau of International Commerce, U.S. Department of Commerce, issues hundreds of publications annually on various topics, many of which are of great value to exporters and those interested in exporting.

Among these publications are:

Checklist of International Business Publications: Basically an index of publications available free from any Department of Commerce District Office.

Overseas Business Reports (OBR): These reports provide basic background data for businessmen who are evaluating various export markets or are considering entering new areas. These reports cover both developing and industrialized countries.

Each OBR discusses separate topics on a single country, such as basic economic data, foreign trade regulations, market factors, selling, establishing a business, plus special statistical reports on U.S. trade with major world areas.

Foreign Economic Trends and Their Implications for the

United States: This series of country-by-country reports gives in-depth reviews of current business conditions, current and near-term prospects, and the latest available data on GNP, foreign trade, wage and price indices, unemployment rates, and construction starts. They are of particular value for their analysis of current developments and their implications for future U.S. trade.

Economic Trends are compiled by the U.S. Embassy Commercial Staff, transmitted to the United States by air, and promptly reproduced for subscribers as soon as they are received from abroad. Available reports are listed by country in the Checklist.

Foreign Market Reports: This series consists of more than 300 reports a month received by the Department of Commerce from specialists in U.S. Foreign Service posts abroad. Individual reports are of such a specialized nature in their coverage of commercial news and developments that they are of primary interest only to specific segments of the U.S. business community and therefore are distributed only on individual request.

They include commodity-oriented reports on production and other developments in the agriculture, manufacturing, mining, fisheries, power and fuels, transportation, distribution and trade, construction and communication fields. The data they provide is particularly valuable in assessing market potentials throughout the world.

The Reports are listed in monthly and cumulative annual indices, and both the reports and the indices are provided without cost in response to specific requests received on business letterheads.

Commerce Today, a news magazine published every other week by the Office of Public Affairs, is the Commerce Department's principal periodical for presentation of domestic and international business news and news of the application of technology to business and industrial problems.

Commerce Business Daily contains a daily synopsis of the U.S. Government procurement invitations, subcontracting leads, contract awards, sales of surplus property, and foreign business opportunities.

Businessmen who wish to personally discuss the export prospects for their products may visit the Department of Commerce in Washington at 14th Street and Constitution Avenue. Appointments will be made for you with export professionals by the Business Counseling Section. Businessmen may also visit any of the Department's 43 District Offices around the country. Each office is staffed with a specialist in international trade who will be glad to assist you.

Information also is available from your State government, either through your State Department of Commerce or State export development agency.

Private Sources

Besides government, there are many private sources of export information including:

Trade associations

Foreign freight forwarders

International Bankers

Local Chambers of Commerce

Customers, suppliers, and other firms producing similar products

You should contact or talk to as many of these sources as possible.

II. SELECTING SALES AND DISTRIBUTION CHANNELS

There are two basic approaches to selling internationally, either direct or indirect. When selling direct, the

American manufacturer deals with a foreign firm and is usually responsible for shipping the products overseas. The indirect method means dealing through another American firm which acts as a sales intermediary and which will normally assume the responsibility for moving the products overseas.

INDIRECT SELLING

There are several different types of intermediary firms and the manufacturer will have to decide on the type of operation he feels will best be able to sell his products.

Commission Agents—Commission or buying agents are "finders" for foreign firms wanting to purchase American products. These purchasing agents obtain the desired equipment at the lowest possible price. A commission is paid to them by their foreign clients.

Country Controlled Buying Agents—These are foreign government agencies or quasi-governmental firms empowered to locate and purchase desired goods.

Export Management Companies—EMCs, as they are called, act as the export department for several manufacturers of non-competitive products. They solicit and transact business in the name of the manufacturers they represent for a commission, salary, or retainer plus commission. They do not buy or sell for their own account, nor do they finance any of the transactions.

This can be an exceptionally fine arrangement for smaller firms which haven't the time, personnel, or money to develop foreign markets, but wish to establish a corporate and product identity internationally.

Export Merchants—The export merchant purchases products direct from the manufacturer and has them packed and marked to his specifications. He then sells overseas through his contacts, in his own name, and assumes all risks for his account.

Export Agents—The export agent operates in the same manner as a manufacturer's representative, but the risk of loss remains with the manufacturer.

In the last two methods the seller is faced with the possible disadvantage of giving up control over the marketing and promotion of his product which could have an adverse effect on future successes.

DIRECT SELLING

The product involved, and the way it is marketed in the United States, will provide a clue on how it might be marketed internationally, i.e. through a representative, stocking distributor, consignment agent, retail store, or even directly to the end user. The customary business methods and established channels of distribution in individual foreign countries will also have a bearing on how to proceed.

Sales Representatives or Agents—A sales representative is the equivalent of a manufacturer's representative here in the United States. Product literature and samples are used to present the product to the potential buyer. He usually works on a commission basis, assumes no risk or responsibility, and is under contract for a definite period of time (renewable by mutual agreement). This contract defines territory, terms of sale, method of compensation, and other details. He may operate on either an exclusive or non-exclusive basis.

Distributor—The foreign distributor is a merchant who purchases merchandise from a U.S. manufacturer at the greatest possible discount and resells it for his profit. This would be the preferred arrangement if the product being sold requires periodic servicing. The prospective distributor should be willing to carry a sufficient parts supply and maintain adequate facilities and personnel to perform all normal servicing operations. Since the distributor buys in his name, it is easier for the U.S. manufacturer to establish a credit pattern so more flexible or convenient payment terms can be offered. As in the case of the sales representative, the length of association is established by contract which is renewable if the arrangement proves satisfactory.

Foreign Retailer—Generally limited to the consumer line, this method relies mainly on direct contact by traveling salesmen but, depending on the product, can also be accomplished by the mailing of catalogs, brochures, or other literature. In using the direct mail approach (while it will eliminate commissions and traveling expenses), the U.S. manufacturer could suffer because his proposal may not receive proper consideration.

Selling Direct to the End User—This is quite limited and again depends on the product. Opportunities often arise from advertisements in magazines receiving overseas distribution. Many times this can create difficulties because the casual inquirer may not be fully cognizant of his country's foreign trade regulations. For several reasons, he may not be able to receive the merchandise upon arrival, thus causing it to be impounded and possibly sold at public auction, or returned on a freight collect basis which could prove to be costly.

State Controlled Trading Companies—This term applies to countries which have state trading monopolies, where business is conducted by a few government sanctioned and controlled trading entities. Because of world-wide changes in foreign policy and their effect on trade between countries, these areas can become important future markets. For the time being, however, most opportunities will be limited to raw materials, agricultural machinery, manufacturing equipment, technical instruments, etc., rather than consumer or household goods. This is due to the shortage of foreign exchange (dollars) and the emphasis on self-sufficiency.

III. COMMUNICATING OVERSEAS

Knowing how to communicate overseas is basic information that every exporter should learn early. Your first contact with a potential customer or an agent in a foreign country will probably be by letter, and letters will continue to be one of your major methods of communication.

Communicating business information abroad by letter does differ considerably from your domestic communications. For this reason, take some time to learn what is generally expected in international business communications.

CHECKLIST FOR LETTERS

Use this checklist as a guide for international business letter writing:

1. Answer overseas inquiries promptly and in the language of the letter of inquiry, when requested.

2. If you are actively doing business overseas, your letterhead should reflect this by including U.S.A. in the address, cable information, and the name of your bank to enable overseas customers to make credit checks with little difficulty.

3. Do not ask for credit information in your first sales letter. This information can best be obtained from other sources such as the international banking department of your own bank, or U.S. Department of Commerce.

4. Make sure your letter adequately introduces your firm and establishes you as a reliable source of supply.

5. Be polite, courteous, and friendly but without undue familiarity and slang. Some overseas firms, particularly those in Latin America, feel the usual brief U.S. business letter is lacking in courtesy.

6. Make sure your letter contains full information about your product, prices, etc., so the customer will not have to ask for further details before ordering.

7. Give adequate information for the buyer to calculate the cost of your product delivered to arrival point in his country (Refer to Chapter VI, Pricing Quotations and Terms of Sale).

8. Better results can be obtained if you use your customer's system of measurement. For example, centimeters instead of inches. You may wish to insert the metric figure or other measurement in parenthesis following the U.S. measurement.

9. Personally sign your letter. Form letters are not satisfactory.

10. Send your letters by airmail and request responses the same way. Make sure you use the correct postage. Many firms fail to check this simple yet important point. Also consider using stamps, instead of a postage meter, to command more attention.

11. Finally, check your letter over to make sure it says what you intend. Remember letters can be good salesmen.

WHAT TO DO WITH AN INQUIRY

Suppose you receive an inquiry from a foreign firm about your product. What actions should you take? Follow this checklist:

1. On receiving an inquiry:

- Check for the correct address of the foreign firm. Don't discard the envelope until you are sure the complete address appears on the firm's letterhead.
- Check nature of inquiry.
- Check type of quotation desired.

2. Acknowledge inquiry if quotation cannot be sent immediately.

3. Compute price according to the terms of quotation (refer to Chapter VI, Pricing, Quotation, and Terms of Sale), and check credit and reputation of customer.

4. When order is received:

- Check order to verify your ability to comply with the terms of the order.
- Acknowledge order and stipulate any deviations or corrections.
- Make sure all personnel involved with processing order fully understand their part.
- If payment is by Letter of Credit (Refer to Chapter VII, Receiving Payment for Your Products), check carefully as soon as it is received and, if you cannot comply, request change immediately.

5. Prepare the order for shipment (Refer to Chapter IX, Preparing Your Products for Foreign Shipment).

6. When date that order is to be ready for shipment is known:

- Contact freight forwarder and arrange shipping schedule (Refer to Chapter X, Shipping Your Products).
- Make sure necessary shipping instructions and documents are completed correctly and distributed on time.

7. Prepare and submit collection documents to receive payment (Refer to Chapter XI, Documenting Your Shipments).

IV. LOCATING FOREIGN REPRESENTATIVES

How does an exporter locate someone in a foreign country who is qualified and interested in handling his product?

DEPARTMENT OF COMMERCE

One of the most effective and economical ways of locating foreign representation is by utilizing the services of the Department of Commerce which has several aids designed to assist the American manufacturer. Some of these are as follows:

The Agent/Distributor Service (ADS)

The ADS is used to seek representatives (agents) and/or distributors. The essence of the service is the determination of a foreign firm's interest in a specific U.S. proposal and willingness to correspond with the U.S. requester. U.S. Foreign Service posts supply up to three selected names of such firms together with the addresses, persons to contact and type of business. Fee for the service is $25.

ADS application forms are obtainable through the Commerce Department District Offices. International trade specialists at these offices will assist applicants in preparing the application. They will give guidance and ascertain that there are no factors barring the desired relationship.

Trade Opportunities Program (TOP)

TOP is an easy, effective way for a U.S. company to learn about overseas firms that could act as agents or distributors for his products (Also see Chapter XIV). The U.S. company, as a subscriber to TOP, specifies the products and the countries for which he would like to receive notices of overseas representation opportunities. That information is put into the TOP computer.

As representation opportunities are telexed to Commerce from Foreign Service posts, they are put into the computer and matched against the subscriber's information specifications. When a match occurs, the computer prints out a notice of the opportunity which is then mailed to the subscriber. The cost of each is 50 cents, chargeable against the subscriber's TOP account. A company can subscribe to TOP for as little as $25.

Export Contact List Services

The Department of Commerce collects and stores information on foreign firms in a master computer file designated the Foreign Traders Index (FTI). The file contains information on over 126,000 importing firms, agents, representatives, distributors, manufacturers, service organizations, retailers, and potential end users of American products and/or services in 114 countries. Newly identified firms are constantly being added to the file while information on previously listed firms is updated frequently. This information is available to U.S. exporters in the following three forms:

A. *Export Mailing List Service (EMLS)*. The EMLS consists of special targeted retrievals for individual requestors wishing to obtain lists of foreign firms in selected countries by commodity classification. Retrievals are offered on gummed mailing labels or on printouts and include, to the extent available, the name and address of the firm, name and title of executive officer, type of organization, year established, relative size, number of employees and salesmen, and product or service codes by SIC number. A $15 "set-up" fee must accompany the request for each retrieval. The basic charge covers payment for 300 or less printed names. An additional 5-cent charge per name is made for each name over the 300 included in the base payment, and is billed direct to the requestor.

B. *FTI Data Tape Service (DTS)*. Through this service, information on all firms included in the FTI for all countries (or in selected countries) is available to U.S. firms on magnetic tape. Users can retrieve various segments of the data in unlimited combinations through their own computer facilities.

C. *Trade Lists*. Following is a brief description of three styles of individually printed, industry Trade Lists that are available from the Department of Commerce.

1. *Target Industry Trade Lists* (See page 41 for explanation of "Target Industry" program). Categorized in accordance with SIC product or service identification codes, these lists provide information similar to that included in the EMLS printouts described above and are available individually for each country in which research was conducted in relation to Target Industry categories.

2. *Lists of "State Controlled Trading Companies."* Identifies government sanctioned and controlled trading entities in those countries where foreign trade is conducted through state-owned or controlled organizations.

3. *Business Firms*. These lists contain the names of all commercial business firms in developing countries.

Note: *The Commodity Trade Lists* which have been published for a number of years on an individual country basis have been discontinued and have been replaced by the EMLS service.

Specialized U.S. Government Trade Missions

Specialized U.S. Government Trade Missions are groups of American businessmen recruited by Commerce from a specific industry to promote the sale of the products or services of that particular industry, or to establish representation in overseas markets. Commerce provides detailed marketing information, advanced planning, publicity, trip coordination, and assumes the expense of mission operations. The Mission members pay their own expenses and conduct business on behalf of the firms they represent.

Commercial Exhibitions

Trade shows, either wholly sponsored by the U.S. Government or in which it is participating, where American products can be displayed at low cost to test a market, generate sales, or locate representation (Refer to Chapter XII, Promoting Product Sales Overseas).

Business Travel Overseas

For firms desiring to travel overseas to search for a qualified business partner and to gain first hand knowledge regarding the country's business condition, U.S. Commercial officers in the American Embassy or Consulate can provide considerable assistance—either by way of in-depth briefings or by arranging introduction to appropriate firms, individuals or foreign government officials. Commerce District Offices should be notified of a pending trip at least 3 weeks prior to the projected arrival date in the foreign country to discuss the purpose of the visit.

If the trip is in conjunction with a particular Commerce program or project and the type of assistance requested is determined to require special preparation by the Foreign Service the American firm will be asked to complete a form giving full particulars of their trip and extent of service desired. This information will then be cabled to the respective overseas Foreign Service posts so they may have sufficient time to take necessary and effective action. To qualify for this "specialized" service the American business traveler must agree to maintain his projected travel schedule or, if unable to do so, notify the affected posts of this inability several days in advance of his scheduled arrival.

All other American businessmen not requiring this "specialized" service will be requested to write direct to the Posts to be visited outlining the purpose of their trip, scheduled itinerary, and type of assistance desired.

Commercial Newsletters

Many of the larger U.S. Embassies and Consulates publish a periodic newsletter which is distributed to the business community they serve. At no cost, it is possible for U.S. firms to have new products described in this publication so that if a local representative is interested, he may contact the American firm.

INDUSTRY ORGANIZATIONS

Private groups (representing a state, city, chamber of commerce, trade association, industry group, or single industry) occasionally sponsor and finance various types of overseas promotions, one of which is Industry Organized Government Approved Trade Missions. An IOGA Trade Mission consists of a group of American businessmen who wish to promote the sale of U.S. products or services, or to establish agents. The U.S. Department of Commerce will assist in planning the Mission and coordinating arrangements with U.S. foreign Service Posts. A Commerce official will brief mission members prior to departure regarding business, economic, and political conditions in the country to be visited.

BANKS

Banks can be another excellent source of assistance. Acting through their own international department or through the international department of an affiliate bank in the States, it is possible for them to locate, through correspondent or branch banks overseas, reputable firms qualified and willing to represent American firms.

SERVICE ORGANIZATIONS

Ocean freight carriers, airlines, port authorities, and American Chambers of Commerce maintain offices throughout the world. Through these offices it is often possible for U.S. firms to find outlets or representation at no cost or obligation.

Many of these same organizations also publish newsletters or booklets that are widely distributed overseas in which products can be described to attract interested representatives.

PUBLICATIONS

There are many foreign circulation business and travel magazines in which advertising space can be purchased to either solicit representation or publicize products.

RELIABILITY

After locating a potential foreign representative, it is necessary to investigate him to assure he is reliable and reputable before entering into an agreement. It is recommended that at least two supporting business and credit reports be obtained. There are several ways this can be accomplished.

1. *World Traders Data Reports.* A business report available from the Department of Commerce which gives such information as the type of organization, year established,

relative size, number of employees, general reputation, territory covered, language preferred, product lines handled, principal owners, financial references, and trade references. It also contains a general narrative report by the U.S. Commercial officer conducting the investigation as to the reliability of the foreign firm. Fee for this service is $15.

2. Commercial credit reporting firms such as Dun & Bradstreet, Foreign Credit Interchange Bureau, and Retail Credit Corporation offer similar data.

3. Another source of credit information is through U.S. banks and their correspondent banks or branches overseas.

V. DRAWING UP AN AGREEMENT WITH YOUR REPRESENTATIVE

After successfully making contact with a prospective representative and investigating his integrity, financial responsibility, community standing, share of the market, other product lines which he represents for conflict of interest, the next step is to consider the foreign sales agreement itself.

BASIC ITEMS

An agreement of this type can be either relatively simple or detailed. The following basic items are normally included in a typical foreign sales agreement:
- The names and addresses of both parties.
- The date when the agreement goes into effect.
- Duration of the agreement.
- Provisions for extending or terminating the agreement.
- Description of product lines included.

- Definition of sales territory.
- Establishment of discount and/or commission schedules and determination of when and how paid.
- Provisions for revising the commission or discount schedules.
- Establishment of a policy governing resale prices.
- Maintenance of appropriate service facilities.
- Restrictions to prohibit the manufacture and sale of similar and competitive products.
- Designation of responsibility for patent and trademark negotiations and/or policing.
- The assignability or non-assignability of the agreement and any limiting factors.
- Designation of the country (not necessarily the United States) and state (if applicable) of contract jurisdiction in the case of dispute.

The agreement should also contain statements to the effect that the representative will not: have business dealings with a competitive firm; reveal any confidential information in a way that would prove injurious, detrimental, or competitive to the American firm; enter into agreements binding on the American firm, and all inquiries received from outside the designated sales territory are to be referred to the American firm for appropriate action.

To insure a conscientious sales effort from the representative on behalf of the American firm, the foreign representative should also agree to devote his utmost skill and ability to the sale of the product for the compensation named in the contract.

For tax purposes, in both the United States and possibly foreign countries as well, the place and time at which title to the merchandise passes from the seller to the buyer can be very important and therefore, in certain instances, should be written into the agreement.

At all times, avoid articles which could be contrary to United States antitrust laws. Legal advice should be sought when preparing and entering into foreign agreements.

VI. PRICING, QUOTATIONS, AND TERMS OF SALE

Pricing your product is very important because the price must be high enough to return a suitable profit yet low enough to be competitive in foreign markets. The price at which you can sell your product also will significantly influence your evaluation of the attractiveness of overseas markets and thus your commitment to selling to them.

DOMESTIC PRICE

The overwhelming majority of new exporters simply use the domestic price plus freight, packing, insurance, etc., forgetting other factors that enter into a C.I.F. quotation. This may result in a price that is too high or occasionally a price that is too low. Export prices should be kept as low as possible, consistent with a reasonable profit. Many experts recommend that domestic marketing costs, such as sales and advertising expenses be eliminated in determining overseas prices.

MARGINAL COST PRICING

The most realistic method of pricing is what is termed marginal cost pricing. This method, based on incremental costs, considers direct out-of-pocket costs of producing and selling products for export as a floor under which prices cannot be set without incurring a loss. Once this is known, you can then take into account competitive prices when setting your own price.

PRODUCT MODIFICATION

Another possibility in pricing is modification of the product so that it can be sold at a competitive price and still yield a reasonable profit. This may involve decreasing the contents of a package or simplification of an elaborate product so that a certain price level can be achieved.

PREPARING YOUR QUOTATION

A quotation basically describes the product, states a price for that product at a specified delivery point, sets the time of shipment, and specifies the terms of payment.

Since the foreign buyer may not be familiar with the product, its description in an overseas quotation must be more detailed than in a domestic one. The description should include the total gross and net shipping weight, total cubic volume packed for export, as well as individual out-to-out dimensions, if possible. This information is necessary so the buyer may determine if any special loading or handling equipment will be required; it will also enable him to compute transportation charges. In some countries the import duties and/or taxes are assessed on the weight of the shipment rather than on the dollar valuation and the buyer must be able to calculate this in advance.

It is important to stipulate whether the material being quoted is new or used. Any options included in the basic quotation should be mentioned as well as other factors that could affect the price.

Many times, a seller is requested to submit a pro forma

invoice with his quotation. These invoices *are not* for payment purposes. They are models only which the buyer will use when applying for an import license or in arranging for funds. When preparing final collection invoices at time of shipment, it is advisable to check with the Department of Commerce or some other reliable source for any special invoicing requirements that may prevail in the country to which you are shipping.

The time of shipment or shipping schedule can be important to a prospective buyer. It should always be specified whether the time quoted for shipment is from the factory or the port of export. The estimated shipping date from the U.S. port of export is always preferable since the overseas buyer has no way of estimating inland transit time in the United States.

TERMS OF SALE

It is very important that a common understanding exists regarding the delivery terms. In the United States it is customary to ship "F.O.B. Factory," "Freight Collect," "Prepay and Charge" or "C.O.D.," but an entirely different set of terms is used in international business, some of which sound similar but have different explanations. A complete listing of definitions is contained in the pamphlet, *Revised American Foreign Trade Definitions,* issued by the National Foreign Trade Council, 10 Rockefeller Plaza, New York, N.Y. 10020. Some of the more common terms used in international trade and a simplified explanation of what they mean are given below:

c.i.f. (cost, insurance, freight) to named overseas port of import. Under this term, the seller quotes a price including the goods, insurance, and all transportation and miscellaneous charges to the point of debarkation from vessel or air-craft.

c.&f. (cost and freight) to named overseas port of import. Under this term, the seller quotes a price including the cost of transportation to the named point of debarkation.

f.a.s. (free along side) at named U.S. port of export. Under this term, the seller quotes a price, including service charges and delivery of the goods along side the vessel.

f.o.b. (free on board). There are a number of classes of F.O.B. Here are three:

    f.o.b. (named inland point of origin)
    f.o.b. (named port of exportation)
    f.o.b. Vessel (named port of export)

Ex (named point of origin) e.g., Ex Factory, Ex Warehouse, etc. Under this term, the price quoted applies only at the point of origin, and seller agrees to place the goods at the disposal of buyer at the agreed place on the date or within the period fixed. All other charges are for the account of the buyer.

In quoting, make your price meaningful. A price for industrial machinery quoted "f.o.b. Saginaw, Michigan, not export packed" would be ignored by prospective foreign buyers. Such buyers would have no way to determine with any accuracy what the export packing costs would be in Saginaw and would not know the freight charges from Saginaw to the port of export.

Always quote c.i.f. whenever possible, this means something abroad. This shows the foreign buyer what it costs to get your product into a port in his country or in a nearby port.

If you need assistance in figuring the c.i.f. price, a freight forwarder will be glad to help you. Furnish him with a description of your product, the weight and cubic measurement when packed. He can then compute the c.i.f. price and usually will not charge you for this service.

VII. RECEIVING PAYMENT FOR YOUR EXPORTS

There are six basic methods of receiving payment for products sold overseas. In many respects, some of them are quite similar to domestic payment terms.

CASH IN ADVANCE

This, of course, is the most desirable method of all since the shipper is relieved of collection problems and has immediate use of the money.

On the other hand, unless it is a very small order the foreign buyer may object to these terms because it ties up his capital until he receives the merchandise and resells it. He may also have reservations as to whether or not he will actually receive his merchandise.

OPEN ACCOUNT

Unless the buyer is of unquestionable integrity (which has been determined through a thorough credit investigation or by prior experience) these terms can be somewhat risky for the seller.

In addition, the exporter's capital is tied up until payment is received, It is a standard practice, in many countries, to wait until the merchandise is received, thus delaying payment even longer.

CONSIGNMENT SALES

The same basic procedure is followed as in the United States. The material is furnished to a foreign concern on a deferred payment basis until they have sold the products and are able to reimburse the seller.

This method is limited to products that lend themselves to an operation of this type.

The countries in which sales of this nature are contemplated should be examined closely for economic and political stability.

It may be wise to consider some form of political risk insurance. In addition, the contractual agreement should establish who will be responsible for property risk insurance covering the merchandise until it is sold and payment is received.

SIGHT DRAFT

This method of shipment is used when the seller wishes to retain control of the shipment, either for credit reasons or for the purpose of title retention. Shipment is made on a negotiable order bill of lading consigned to either the order of the shipper or to a third party. The original order bill of lading must be properly endorsed by the bearer and surrendered to the carrier before the cargo can be released.

In actual practice, the original order bill of lading is endorsed by the shipper and sent to the buyer's bank along with a sight draft, invoices, and other necessary supporting documents specified either by the buyer or his country, e.g., packing lists, consular invoices, insurance certificates, and inspection certificates. The bank notifies the buyer that they have received these documents, and as soon as he pays the amount of the draft he will get the bill of lading enabling him to obtain his shipment.

A certain degree of risk remains with this manner of shipment because the buyer's financial position may change between the time the goods are shipped and the time the drafts are presented for payment. Also, the political policies of the importing country may change.

TIME DRAFTS

With the time draft, the buyer can obtain possession of the goods when he accepts the draft and defer payments for 30, 60, 90 days or even longer.

DELIVERY ORDERS

Some countries do not recognize or permit sight draft shipments involving negotiable bills of lading. In these instances, in order to protect themselves, shippers may consign the merchandise to a third party such as an import broker in the foreign country on a straight bill of lading. The shipper will then write a letter called a "delivery order" to the third party authorizing him to release the shipment to the bearer on the original delivery order. The original delivery order is sent to the buyer's bank with a draft and other supporting documents required by that country. Included are instructions to the effect that original delivery order addressed to the broker be released to the buyer only after they have honored or accepted the draft, whichever the case may be.

Since there are no negotiable air bills of lading, a similar arrangement can be used to protect air shipments. This also applies to parcel post shipments. In these instances, the third party is usually the buyer's bank. Approval must be obtained from the bank prior to shipment to ensure that it is acceptable and to prevent later difficulties.

LETTERS OF CREDIT

A frequently used form of collection is payment against a letter of credit. This is a document, issued by a bank at the buyer's request in favor of the seller, promising to pay the agreed amount of money upon receipt by the bank of certain documents within a specified time. These documents are usually the same as those furnished for a sight draft collection.

Letters of credit may be revocable or irrevocable, but preferably are irrevocable. This means that once the credit has been accepted by the seller, it cannot be altered in any way by the buyer without the permission of the seller.

It is also most desirable to have the buyer confirm the letter of credit through a U.S. bank. By doing this the U.S. bank is accepting the responsibility to pay, regardless of the financial situation of the buyer or foreign bank. This is a definite advantage because the seller can receive payment as soon as the documents are presented to the bank.

Normally, on all transactions handled through banks, the collection charges (fees collected by both the foreign and U.S. banks for their services) are charged to the account of the drawee (buyer) and should be so stated in all quotations and on all drafts.

These are the basic methods of obtaining payment but there are several variations to each that can apply, such as acceptance drafts, documentary payment orders, authority to pay, etc. Additional information can be obtained from banks with international departments, or from any U.S. Department of Commerce District Office.

VIII. Financing Exports

There are many sources of financial assistance available to exporters. First, of course, is your own working capital or bank line of credit. Use of your own facilities may, however, restrict your total cash availability even if you were to establish a separate export line of credit with your bank.

COMMERCIAL BANKS

You have a wide choice of financial institutions that are prepared to provide international financing and marketing assistance to exporters. More than 200 U.S. banks have qualified international banking departments with specialists familiar with particular foreign countries and experts in different types of commodities and transactions. These banks, located in all major U.S. cities, maintain correspondent relationships with smaller banks throughout the United States. This banking network enables any exporter to find assistance (for himself or his overseas customer) for his export financing needs. The larger banks also maintain correspondent relationships with banks in most foreign countries or operate their own overseas branches, providing a direct channel to overseas customers.

FACTORING HOUSES

Exporters should also be aware of factoring houses that deal in accounts receivable of American exporters. Although possibly charging higher fees, they will purchase your receivables, often without recourse, assuring you of prompt payment for your export sale.

EXPORT MANAGEMENT COMPANIES

Export management companies will not only act as your export representative, but some of these professional export houses will also carry the financing for the export sale, again assuring you of immediate payment and removing from your company any foreign credit risk.

EXIMBANK

The U.S. Government also participates in the financing of America's exports. The Export-Import Bank of the United States (Eximbank) offers direct loans for large projects and equipment sales that usually require longer term financing. It also cooperates with commercial banks in the United States and abroad in providing a number of financial arrangements to help U.S. exporters offer credit to their overseas buyers. Eximbank also provides export credit guarantees to commercial banks that in turn finance export sales; and, through the Foreign Credit Insurance Association (FCIA), provides insurance to American exporters which enables them to extend credit terms to their overseas buyers. In all cases, the Bank must find a "reasonable assurance of repayment" as a precondition of participating in the transaction.

Eximbank's medium-term guarantee program primarily relates to the sale of capital goods, i.e., industrial and agricultural equipment, and other products normally sold on repayment terms of 181 days to 5 years. Longer terms may be granted in exceptional situations.

Under this program, the foreign buyer is required to make a cash payment of at least 10% of the contract price and the exporter must carry at his own risk at least 10% of the financial portion of the sale throughout the term of the credit. In some cases, these percentages may be higher. These guarantees require the U.S. commercial banks to finance the sale without recourse to the exporter except for that percentage of the financed portion the exporter must carry for his own account.

Eximbank also has a Cooperative Financing Facility which extends financing to many thousands of customers of financial institutions outside the United States. Under this program, Eximbank lends to a cooperating financing institution one-half the funds required for a purchase from the United States, after a cash payment of at least 10%. The cooperating institution, in turn, lends the full amount of the financing to its customer.

Under the Cooperative Financing Facility, Eximbank supports the export of capital goods, components and spare parts for buyers and sellers who might otherwise have no access to such financing. Since the indigenous commercial bank takes all the commercial risk, approval of an export transaction is handled by Eximbank within a span of two days. Potential exporters should familiarize themselves with the names and locations of the hundreds of banks overseas who are prepared to finance their sales in nearly every country in the free world.

Eximbank also operates a Relending Facility similar to the Cooperative Financing Facility. Under this program, which is being phased out in most countries, Eximbank lends to a relending institution the full amount of the funds required for purchases of a very few selected product lines for which the U.S. market share is unduly low.

Eximbank regulations and conditions of assistance are, of course, subject to change. For more information, consult your commercial bank, or write directly to the Export-Import Bank of the United States, 811 Vermont Avenue, N.W., Washington, D.C. 20571.

FOREIGN CREDIT INSURANCE ASSOCIATION

In the highly competitive international business world the ability of an exporter to offer terms to his customer often may mean the difference between winning or losing the sale. Exporters accustomed to selling for cash with order or a confirmed irrevocable letter-of-credit basis are finding it increasingly necessary to offer terms that may run from cash against documents, to time drafts, open account, or installment payments spread over a number of years. The export credit insurance offered by FCIA provides an incentive to American exporters to offer competitive terms to their buyers.

The FCIA administers the U.S. export credit insurance program on behalf of its member insurance companies and the government owned Eximbank. The private insurers cover the normal commercial credit risks, mainly the insolvency of or the prolonged payment default by the overseas buyer. Eximbank assumes all liability for the political risks, including, in addition to exchange transfer delay, such hazards as war, revolution, or similar hostilities; unforeseen withdrawal or nonrenewal of a license to export or import; requisition, expropriation, confiscation, or intervention in the business of the buyer by a governmental authority; transport or insurance charges caused by interruption or diversion of shipment; and certain other governmental acts which may prevent or unduly delay payment and which are beyond the control of the seller or the buyer.

One of FCIA's major forms of coverage is the master policy, designed to provide under one policy substantially automatic coverage for all of an exporter's sales to overseas buyers on credit terms ranging up to 5 years. The policy may provide political risks coverage only, or comprehensive risks coverage.

To meet special needs, a small business policy is available for businesses new to the export field or whose average annual export volume over the last 3 years did not exceed $200,000. This policy may remain in force for a period not to exceed 2 years or until the insured has covered $500,000 aggregate contract value of exports, at which time conversion to a more conventional policy would be appropriate. For information on other types of policies offered by FCIA, exporters should consult with that Association which is headquartered at One World Trade Center, 9th Floor, New York, New York 10048.

OTHER ORGANIZATIONS

Other organizations which offer forms of export financing assistance include the Overseas Private Investment Corporation (OPIC), Washington, D.C. 20527, and Private Export Funding Corporation (PEFCO), 40 Wall Street, New York, New York 10005.

OPIC offers guarantees comparable to those offered by FCIA and Eximbank to U.S. manufacturers who wish to establish a plant in another country either by themselves or as a joint venture with local capital.

PEFCO, composed of a number of U.S. private banks and exporting companies, makes funds available, with Eximbank's guarantee, for financing long-term credits to U.S. customers. Through PEFCO, these companies allocate a certain amount of their resources for credit investments they would not make normally because of the length of time their funds would be tied up.

IX. PREPARING YOUR PRODUCTS FOR FOREIGN SHIPMENT

There are four distinct phases involved in readying a shipment for movement overseas.

ENGINEERING

It may be necessary to introduce some modifications to a product to successfully enter a foreign market, in order to conform with country regulations, historical preferences, local customs, to facilitate movement, reduce costs, or to compensate for possible differences in electrical current and/or measurement standards.

1. Many foreign countries use different electrical standards than those in the United States. It is not unusual to find phase, cycle, or voltages, both in home and commercial usage overseas, that would damage equipment designed for use in the United States, or that would impair its operating efficiency. These will sometimes vary even within a given country. This knowledge will let the exporter know if it is necessary to substitute a special motor and/or arrange for a different drive ratio to achieve a desirable operating RPM or service factor.

2. Many items of equipment must be graduated in the metric system to allow them to be integrated with other pieces of equipment or to allow work to be completed in the standard of a country.

3. As freight charges are usually assessed on a weight or volume basis, whichever provides the greater revenue for the carrier, some consideration must be given to shipping an item disassembled, rather than assembled, in order to lower delivery costs. Also, this may be necessary to facilitate movement on narrow roads, streets, through doorways or elevators which could otherwise cause transit problems.

4. Local customs or historical preference regarding size, color, speed, source, or grade of raw materials, etc., are other reasons why a redesign might be considered. In addition, many foreign governments have established mandatory standards. These will usually be specified with the request for quotation.

PRODUCTION

The most important thing to remember here is to process overseas orders as promptly as a domestic order rather than wait for a slack period. It is much more difficult to explain, in a different language, to someone halfway around the world, the reason for a delayed shipment than to someone locally. If a shipment is delayed, it may be necessary to extend the expiration date of a letter of credit. This is an added expense to the buyer, one he won't appreciate, especially if it happens often.

PACKING

Considerable attention should be given to the actual preparation of the merchandise for overseas movement. The condition of the merchandise when it arrives, plus the overall cost of the shipment will reflect how much consideration was given to this important subject.

There are four problems that must be kept in mind when designing an export shipping crate: Breakage, weight, moisture, and pilferage. In addition to the normal handling experienced in a domestic movement, an export order moving by ocean freight will be loaded aboard a vessel by use of a sling, in a net with other items, by conveyor, chute, or other method, putting added stress and strain on the package. In the hold of a ship other cargo may be stacked on top of the order or come in violent contact with it during the course of the voyage. At the overseas destination, the handling facilities may not be as sophisticated as in the United States and the cargo may be dragged, pushed, rolled, and dropped during the unloading, while moving in and out of customs, or in transit to the final destination.

Moisture is a constant problem as the cargo is subject to condensation in the hold of a ship, even one equipped with air conditioning and a dehumidifier. The cargo may be unloaded in the rain and many foreign ports do not have covered storage facilities.

Unless the cargo is adequately protected, theft and pilferage are always constant threats. One deterrent to pilferage is to avoid mention of the contents or trade names on the package. Strapping and seals also discourage theft. Another very effective means of eliminating moisture and pilferage is shrink wrapping. This involves sealing the merchandise in a plastic film.

Some tips: Heavy crates should be skidded and have provisions for fork lift trucks; they should have notches to facilitate the use of slings; cement-coated nails are recommended because they hold better; packages should be strapped since this gives added strength; plywood sheathing is economical and strong; avoid overpacking since customs duties in several countries are assessed on the gross weight of the package rather than the value of the merchandise; also, added weight due to overpacking will result in higher inland freight charges both here and at the destination, not to mention the cost of the packing itself.

Waterproofing can also be achieved by using waterproof inner liners, moisture absorbing agents, and by coating finished metal parts with special rust inhibitors.

One increasingly popular method of shipment is the use of "containers" which can be obtained from carriers or private concerns. These will vary in size, material, and construction, can accommodate most cargo but are more readily suitable to standard size and shaped packages. Some containers are no more than truck bodies that are lifted off their wheels and placed on a vessel at the port of export, then transferred to another set of wheels at the port of import for movement to an inland destination.

Shipments by air, as a rule, do not require as heavy

packing as do ocean shipments but still must be adequately protected. In many cases the standard domestic packing is acceptable, especially if the product is durable in nature and there is no concern for display packaging. In other instances, high test (at least 250 pound psi) cardboard or tri-wall construction boxes are more than adequate.

In the case of both ocean and air shipment, the carriers can advise on the best packaging. Marine insurance companies are also available for consultation on this matter. In the event a firm is not equipped to package for export, there are professional firms that will undertake this at moderate cost.

MARKING

Usually the buyer will specify special export marks that he wishes to appear on the cargo to facilitate identification upon arrival. These "marks" will also help the carriers identify the cargo to insure that it arrives at the correct destination.

Legibility is of utmost importance. Letters should be a minimum of 2" high, stenciled in black waterproof ink, and fully exposed.

As mentioned previously, avoid showing trademarks or other clues that indicate the contents of the cargo in order to avoid pilferage.

Packages should be marked on at least two adjacent sides, and preferably the top also. Sacks should be marked on both sides prior to filling. Drums should be marked on both the side and top.

Old marks should be completely obliterated to avoid confusion. If new marks are to go on over old, care should be taken to use a light color mark-over paint or ink. It should be completely dry before applying the new marks.

In addition to port marks, customer identification code, and indication of origin, the marks should include the package number, gross and net weights, and dimensions. Include any special handling instructions on the package. It is a good idea to repeat these instructions in the language of the country of destination. Standard international shipping and handling symbols should also be utilized.

X. Shipping Your Products

One of the first things you will want to do before shipping your products is arrange for the services of a foreign freight forwarder.

FOREIGN FREIGHT FORWARDER

The foreign freight forwarder acts as an agent for the exporter in moving the cargo to the overseas destination. With few exceptions (air shipments, overland shipments to Canada, or shipments to Hawaii and Puerto Rico) it is recommended that a freight forwarder, licensed by the Federal Maritime Administration, move this cargo from the U.S. port of export. These agents are familiar with the import rules and regulations of foreign countries, methods of shipping, U.S. Government export regulations, and with the documents connected with foreign trade.

They can assist with an order from the start by advising the exporter of the freight costs, port charges, consular fees, cost of any special documentation, insurance costs, as well as their handling fees which will enable him to prepare his quotation. They can also recommend the degree of packing that should be considered to ensure the arrival of the merchandise at the destination in good condition. If desired, they can even arrange to have the merchandise packed at the port of export or to have it containerized.

After the order is ready to ship, they will review the letter of credit, packing list, etc., to ensure that everything is in order. If desired, they can reserve the necessary space aboard an ocean vessel.

When the cargo arrives at the port of export, the forwarders make the necessary arrangements to clear it through Customs and have it delivered to the pier in time for loading aboard the selected vessel. They may also prepare the ocean bill of lading and any special consular documentation which may be required. After shipment, they forward all the documents direct to the customer, or to the paying bank with instructions to credit the exporter's account accordingly.

The cost for their services is a legitimate export cost, and as such may be figured into the contract price charged to the customer.

Freight forwarders may also represent shippers on air freight shipments and perform many of the same services as on an ocean shipment because the procedures and documents involved in both modes of shipment are quite similar.- (NOTE: Although most forwarders' rates and services will be competitive, some even regulated by Federal law, it is recommended that several different bids be obtained as there may be some variations in price. For a fair rate comparison make certain that all of the services being compared are equal.)

EXPORT PACKING LISTS

An export packing list is considerably more detailed and informative than a standard domestic packing list. It itemizes the material in each individual package, and indicates the type of package, i.e., whether a box, crate, drum, bag, etc. It shows the individual net, legal, tare, and gross weights and measurements for each package. In the event shipment is to a country using a different weight and measurement system, the packing list should indicate the packaged dimensions and weights in that system. Package markings should be shown along with the shipper's and buyer's references. If the packing list requires more than one page, the additional pages should be serially numbered and contain a recapitulation on the last page.

A packing list should be either included in or attached to the outside of one package in a waterproof envelope marked "packing list enclosed."

The completed export packing list is used by the shipper, or his forwarding agent, to ascertain the total shipping weight and volume so that shipping space may be reserved. It is also used at the port of export as a checkoff list to determine that the correct cargo has been received.

The export packing list is used by the Customs officials at both the U. S. port of export and the foreign port of import to check the cargo. Finally, it is used by the buyer to inventory the merchandise received.

DOMESTIC SHIPMENT TO THE PORT OF EXPORT

The inland transportation of an export order is handled in much the same way as a domestic one. The export marks should be added to the standard information shown on a domestic bill of lading and, in the case of an ocean shipment, it is also helpful to show the name of the exporting carrier and the latest allowed arrival date at the port of export. Instructions for the inland carrier to notify the exporter's foreign freight forwarder by telephone upon arrival, should also be included so that final delivery arrangements can be made.

For the purpose of export control, a special anti-diversion or destination control statement must also appear on the inland bill of lading. There are three different statements which may be used and which will be discussed in the chapter on documentation.

It should be noted that it is possible to obtain a special export rate, which can result in an appreciable saving in freight charges, when shipping via rail to certain ports. Your freight forwarder can advise on this.

On rail carload shipments to certain countries in the Far East originating east of the Rocky Mountains, it is possible to arrange for a "through bill of lading" from the U. S. point of origin all the way to the destination. There are several advantages to this type of shipment, the most notable being a reduction in the ocean freight rate and the fact that the carriers will absorb the U. S. West Coast wharfage and handling costs levied by the ports.

Another point to keep in mind when making LTL (less than truckload) or LCL (less than carload) shipments: due to ICC rulings, the export cargo must be loaded last so it is the first cargo unloaded. When loading combination shipments of export orders, the vessel sailing dates and loading times must be taken into consideration in order to save time and cost at the port of export.

Arrangements for cargo space on an ocean vessel may be made by the exporter or by his foreign freight forwarder. After reviewing the order requirements regarding shipping dates, destination, and possible routing instructions, and determining the total shipping weight and volume, it then becomes a matter of locating an ocean carrier that best fits the need.

All ocean carriers publish sailing schedules and it is a simple matter to be included on their mailing lists. There are several publications which contain consolidated sailing schedules for all carriers from which it is possible to locate potential carriers who can then be contacted to ascertain if space is available.

OCEAN CARRIERS

There are three basic types of ocean service available to exporters: Conference lines, independent lines, and tramp vessels.

An ocean freight conference is an association of ocean carriers who have joined together in order to establish common freight rates and shipping conditions. They often operate under a dual rate system whereby if an exporter wishes to become a member he is able to ship his cargo at a lower rate than an exporter who is not a member. For this consideration the exporter promises to ship all or a large perecentage of his cargo on vessels of member lines; however, if there is no conference service within a reasonable time to the destination in question, it is possible to ship on an independent's vessel after first obtaining permission from the conference.

Independent lines operate and quote rates individually. They do not require the signing of a dual rate contract as do the conference lines, and will accept bookings from all shippers contingent upon the availability of space. When they are in competition with a conference line, the independent line will usually quote rates approximately 10% lower than the conference lines rates for non-contract shippers.

Both of the above modes of transportation operate on regular established schedules on most world trade routes. On the other hand, the third method of shipment, tramp vessels, are not on an established schedule. However, they usually carry only bulk cargoes.

THE BOOKING CONTRACT

The selected carrier will issue what is known as a "booking contract" which reserves space for the cargo on that vessel. The carrier reserves the right to charge the exporter for this reserved space in the event he fails to use it or to cancel the booking far enough in advance of sailing so the carrier can rebook the space and avoid a revenue loss.

This booking contract may be made by either the exporter or his foreign freight forwarder.

CARGO INSURANCE

Export shipments are usually insured by what is known as ocean marine cargo insurance which insures shipments against loss or damage in transit. While similar to domestic cargo insurance, ocean marine cargo insurance coverage is much broader and, contrary to its name, applies to shipments by mail, or air, as well as by ship.

Ocean marine cargo insurance may be arranged by either the buyer or seller, depending on the terms of sale. However, it should be noted that if the buyer arranges for the insurance, it is very difficult to be certain the coverage is adequate, and, in the event a disaster occurs, the seller might have difficulty in obtaining payment.

Ocean marine cargo insurance is available in two basic forms:

1. A special (one-time) cargo policy that insures a single specific cargo shipment.

2. An open (or blanket) cargo policy which is in

continuous effect and automatically insures all cargo moving at the seller's risk.

The one-time cargo policy is of course more expensive on a per shipment basis since the risk cannot be spread over a number of different shipments. However, if the seller's export business is infrequent, it would be more feasible to utilize the one-time coverage.

XI. DOCUMENTING YOUR SHIPMENTS

Documentation is very important in processing an export order. Special care should be taken in the preparation of the documents to avoid difficulties at time of shipment or collection which could result in delayed payment. Export documentation is divided into two categories—shipping and collection.

SHIPPING DOCUMENTS

These are documents prepared by the shipper or his forwarder to move the shipment through Customs, allow it to be loaded aboard a carrier, and to be shipped to the foreign destination. Included in the shipping document category are packing lists and domestic bills of lading which have already been discussed in Chapter X. The remaining shipping documents of major concern to shippers are as follows:

Export Licenses—Except for areas not subject to U.S. Government Export Administration Laws, all items exported are subject to an export license. This is a permit to allow particular merchandise to be exported. There are two general groups of licenses—Validated Licenses and General Licenses.

Validated Export Licenses

For reasons of strategic significance, short supply, or foreign policy, the United States controls the export movement of certain commodities, and it is necessary to obtain a Validated Export License for each order from the Office of Export Administration in Washington. This requirement can apply on shipments of certain commodities to all countries.

Examples of items that fall into this category are certain chemicals, special types of plastics, sophisticated electronic and communication equipment, and scarce materials such as copper. Articles of war, i.e., arms, ammunition, and military conveyances, fall under the licensing jurisdiction of the Department of State.

General Licenses

General Licenses, and there are several types, are published authorizations which are used to cover the exportation of commodities not subject to validated license. The majority of items shipped overseas fall into one of these general classifications. It is not necessary to submit a formal application or receive written authorizations to ship these products; they can be shipped by merely inserting the correct General License symbol on the export control document known as the Shipper's Export Declaration.

Before an order is quoted, it is wise to check with a Department of Commerce District Office to determine which type of export license is appropriate for that country. If a validated license is required, there are special forms which must generally be supplied by the purchaser or the government of that country to support the request for an export license, and it is well to request these forms in advance to avoid delays. Before applying for an export license, however, it is necessary to actually have received an order.

After the required forms and order are received, an Application for Export License, Form 622-P (formerly FC-419), is prepared along with an Order Processing Card, Form FC-420, and submitted to the Office of Export Administration. If everything is in order, a Validated Export License will generally be issued, usually within two to four weeks.

If an item is not under control, no formal application is necessary and the Department of Commerce District Office can advise as to the correct General License to use in the export documents. Check with the nearest Commerce District Office for assistance on export regulation problems.

Shipper's Export Declaration, Form 7525-V—This document has a dual purpose. First it is the export administration document used in moving the shipment through U.S. Customs. Secondly, it is the source of statistical information which appears in FT-410 which was discussed previously.

This form, in addition to relative shipping information, contains a description of the merchandise being shipped in a certain nomenclature, both written and by a specific commodity identifying number known as a Schedule "B" number.

It is on this document that reference to a specific validated or general export license must appear. It is this identifying nomenclature and reference to the export license that Customs requires before allowing merchandise to leave the country.

In addition, a destination control statement or anti-diversion clause must be shown. This statement must be repeated on the domestic as well as ocean and airway bills of lading, and the invoice. There are three different clauses which may be used, but the one suitable for most general license shipments is: "United States law prohibits disposition of these commodities to Southern Rhodesia, North Korea,

Communist controlled areas of Vietnam or Cuba." This statement permits distribution and resale to all destinations of the world other than these specifically excepted. Additional information on the three statements may be obtained from any Department of Commerce District Office.

COLLECTION DOCUMENTS

These are the documents which are submitted to the customer or his bank in order to receive payment. Collection documents may vary from country to country in method of receiving payment and mode of shipping. Documents may even vary from customer to customer.

Commercial Invoices—As in a domestic shipment, good business practice dictates that a commercial invoice include the full address of the shipper, seller, and consignee, if different; the respective reference numbers; date of the order; shipping date; mode of shipment; delivery and payment terms; a complete description of the merchandise; prices, discounts, and quantities.

In addition, on an export order, it is customary to indicate the origin of the goods, and the export marks. As stated previously, the anti-diversion clause must be shown. If payment is to be against a letter of credit, reference to the bank and the corresponding credit or advice numbers must be given.

Some countries require a special certification, sometimes in the language of that country, incorporated in the invoice. Information about these statements may be obtained from any Department of Commerce District Office.

In some instances, it is necessary for the seller to sign his invoices and even have them notarized or countersigned by his Chamber of Commerce, or both. Many times it is also necessary to have them visaed by the resident consul of the country of destination. Again, this information may be obtained from Department of Commerce District Offices.

Consular Invoices—A few foreign countries, notably Latin American, require a special form of invoice in addition to the commercial invoice. These documents must be prepared in the language of their country and on official forms sold by the respective Consulates. They are then visaed by resident consul thereby certifying to their authenticity and correctness. It is recommended that the shipper's forwarder prepare these documents at time of shipment.

Certificates of Origin—Even though the commercial invoice may contain a statement of origin of the merchandise, a few countries require a separate certificate, sometimes counter-signed by a Chamber of Commerce and possibly even visaed by their resident consul at the port of export. These may be on a special form of the foreign government, while in other cases, a certificate on the shipper's own letterhead will suffice. Statements of origin are required to establish possible preferential rates of import duties under a most favored nation arrangement.

Inspection Certificates—In order to protect themselves, many foreign firms request a certificate of inspection. This may be either an affidavit by the shipper or by an independent inspection firm, as dictated by the buyer, certifying to the quality, quantity, and conformity of goods in relation to the order.

Bills of Lading—These may be overland (truck or rail), air, or ocean bills of lading, depending on destination or terms of sale. As in a domestic shipment, there are two basic types—"straight" or non-negotiable and negotiable or "shipper's order" bills of lading. The latter is used for sight draft or letter of credit shipments. The shipper must endorse the original copy of the "Order" bill of lading before it is presented to the bank for collection. The endorsement may either be "in blank" or "to the order of" a third party such as the negotiating bank. The letter of credit will stipulate which endorsement to use. With the exception of ocean shipments, only one original bill of lading is issued by the carrier. Any number of original ocean bills of lading may be issued depending upon the requirements of the buyer. Normally all original copies are endorsed and submitted to the bank.

According to rules set forth by the International Chambers of Commerce governing foreign trade terms, documents, etc., on draft or letter of credit shipments, the only bill of lading that is acceptable is one that is marked "CLEAN ON BOARD" which means that the carrier has not taken any exception to the condition of the cargo or packing and that the merchandise has actually been loaded aboard the carrying vessel.

Dock Receipts, Warehouse Receipts, Etc.—In cases where the shipper is not responsible for moving the merchandise to the foreign destination, but to the U.S. port of export instead, these documents may be requested. They are exactly as their name implies, a receipt to the effect that the stipulated merchandise has been received at the pier or a warehouse for further disposition.

Certificate of Manufacture—This document is used when a buyer intends to pay for the goods prior to shipment but the lead time for the manufacture of the products is lengthy and the buyer does not desire to allocate the money so far in advance. If the seller feels that the buyer is a good credit risk, he will proceed with the manufacture of the products with perhaps only a down payment. After the merchandise is ready, the seller prepares a certificate stating that the ordered goods have been produced in accordance with the contract and have been set aside for the account of the buyer. Commercial invoices and packing lists are sent as supporting documents. As soon as payment and shipping instructions have been received, the merchandise is shipped.

Insurance Certificates—Where the seller provides ocean marine insurance, it is necessary to furnish insurance certificates, usually in duplicate, indicating the type and amount of coverage involved. Here again, these are negotiable documents and must be endorsed before submitting them to the bank.

The seller can arrange to obtain an open cargo policy to cover all of his foreign shipments or he can use the open cargo policy which his forwarder maintains.

These are the basic documents involved in foreign shipments, however a country or individual buyer may require additional ones and they will be specified either in the order or letter of credit. Special care should be taken when reviewing the order or letter of credit to assure that all of the documents required are furnished in the manner prescribed to avoid rejection and other difficulties.

As mentioned previously, freight forwarders as well as other traffic management firms, are capable and willing to prepare these documents for the shipper at moderate cost.

Another word of caution, shipping documents must be presented for collection within certain time limits after shipment or they will be considered "stale" and the bank will reject them. It will then be necessary to contact the buyer for permission to honor these late documents before the bank will release payment. It is equally important to make sure the shipment is made within the specified time indicated in the letter of credit, otherwise the credit will expire and it may not be possible to receive payment. In most cases it will be possible to arrange for the buyer to pay for the shipment but serious delays may be experienced.

Information regarding the documents required and assistance in their preparation may be obtained from any Department of Commerce District Office.

There is some relief in sight for American businessmen burdened by international documentation. In order to reduce the volume of paperwork, the U.S. Government has been cooperating with the National Committee on International Trade Documentation (NCITD) and other private organizations. A number of documents have been eliminated entirely or their contents incorporated in other required documents. For example, only about 15 countries at the time of this writing still require consular invoices. It is expected that this documents will be eliminated completely in the near future.

A new system called the "U.S. Standard Master for International Trade" has standardized international shipping and collection forms so that all necessary documents required to process a specific shipment can be reproduced from a single master. This has resulted in considerable savings.

Furthermore, there are efforts underway to eliminate documents requiring preparation in the language of the destination country.

Also, many firms are taking advantage of a reporting procedure whereby information regarding all export orders over a 30-day period is filed with the government only once a month instead of on separate Shippers Export Declarations each time a shipment is made.

Finally, to simplify and speed the preparation and processing of all documents and facilitate use of ADP or data transmission systems and equipment, standard universal transportation and commodity descriptions and code systems are being developed.

Information regarding the documents required and assistance in their preparation may be obtained from any Department of Commerce District Office.

XII. Promoting Product Sales Overseas

There are many ways you can promote overseas sales of your products. This may include advertising in magazines and newspapers, radio and TV commercial spots, participation in international trade fairs and U.S. Trade Center exhibitions, or a combination of these.

PROMOTION IN PUBLICATIONS

A large and varied assortment of magazines covering international markets is available to U.S. exporters through American publishers. These range from specialized international magazines that relate to individual industries such as construction, beverages, textiles, and many others to worldwide industrial magazines covering many industries. There is also a wide variety of consumer publications produced by U.S.-based publishers. Many of these publications are produced in national language editions (Spanish for Latin America, etc.) and also offer "regional buys" for specific export markets of the world.

Moreover, these publishers frequently supply potential exporters with helpful market information; make specific recommendations for selling the markets they cover; help advertisers locate sales representation, and render other services to aid the international advertiser.

A complete listing of these international publications can be found in the "International Section" of Standard Rate and Data Service publications (5201 Old Orchard Road, Skokie, Illinois 60076).

TV, radio, and specially produced motion pictures are also used to more or lesser degrees depending on the country. In areas where illiteracy may be high and programs may be seen and heard in public places they offer one of the few means of bringing an advertising message to great numbers of people.

In Latin America, particularly, various forms of outdoor advertising—billboards, posters, electric signs, streetcar and bus cards—are widely used to reach the mass audience.

Because of the specialized knowledge required to advertise and promote successfully in foreign markets, you will probably want to use the services of a U. S. advertising agency with offices or correspondents abroad.

Some U. S. agencies handle nothing but foreign advertising, and some marketing consultants specialize in the problems particular to selling in foreign markets.

The International Advertising Association, Inc., 475 Fifth Avenue, New York, N. Y. 10017, is a good source of names of domestic agencies that handle overseas accounts.

INTERNATIONAL TRADE FAIRS

Sometimes it is difficult to sell a product, depending on its nature, if the potential buyer is unable to physically examine it. Sales letters and brochures are beneficial but it is impossible to judge the quality or sturdiness of an item unless it can be examined. This is made possible through participation in an international trade fair or U. S. Department of Commerce Trade Center exhibition.

In today's commercial world, trade fairs are shopwindows in which thousands of firms from many countries display their products. They are marketplaces in which buyer and seller meet. Many of the long established fairs, especially in Europe, have a history that goes back centuries. More than 800 general and specialized international trade fairs are held each year.

Because the cost of exhibiting overseas on an individual

basis usually prohibits this type of promotion by many firms, the Department of Commerce sponsors an official U.S.A. participation in major international exhibitions. And, in areas where there are no suitable trade fairs, Commerce sponsors special solo exhibitions of American products. Such exhibitions are scheduled only when in-depth research reveals excellent sales potential for these products.

More important, U. S. business firms participating in these Commerce sponsored events receive a full range of promotional and display assistance, all for a moderate participation contribution.

U.S. TRADE CENTER EXHIBITIONS

U. S. Trade Centers offer exporters an excellent device for display, promotion and sale of their products. The Trade Centers are overseas "merchandise marts" or commercial showrooms, established in major marketing centers with high potential for sales of U.S. products.

Commerce currently operates a network of 17 Trade Centers, including a number in strategically located developing markets. Centers are located in Beirut, Buenos Aires, Frankfurt, London, Mexico City, Milan, Osaka, Paris, Seoul, Singapore, Sydney, Stockholm, Taipei, Tehran, Tokyo, Vienna and Warsaw.

From six to nine major product exhibitions are held annually at each center, featuring the displays of about 30 exhibitors. Immediate sales at a show can run as high as $1 million with follow-up sales totaling as much as $20 million over the next 12 months.

Each exhibition is built around a product theme, selected on the basis of market research, that indicates a need for and acceptance of the product, and also identifies the audience for the exhibition. Technical seminars, often held in conjunction with exhibitions, further stimulate interest in the products and help boost sales.

A market promotion campaign is conducted prior to each exhibition by the Trade Center staff. This includes identification of all prospective customers, agents, etc., in the marketing area, publicity in selected media, and individual sales calls on the most promising sales prospects, on behalf of each exhibitor. Total prospect lists vary from market-to-market, but, on the average, each list contains from 6,000 to 20,000 names, all of which are invited to the show by direct mailings and/or personal calls.

The cost to participating U.S. firms is moderate. The exhibitor ships his display products to the exhibition and provides a representative to staff his booth. His only other cost is a participation contribution.

In addition to the pre-show promotional services, the Department of Commerce will:

- Provide exhibit space.
- Design and construct the exhibit.
- Advise on shipment of products to the site.
- Unpack and position display.
- Supply all utilities and housekeeping services.
- Provide a lounge or meeting rooms for exhibitor-customer conferences.
- Provide all necessary show hospitality.
- Pay the cost of returning unsold show exhibit items to the United States.

Here is all a U.S. company must do to participate in a Commerce sponsored exhibition:

- Provide products for display.
- Supply technical and promotional handout literature.
- Ship the products to the exhibition site.

- Assign a representative qualified to man the booth and transact business.
- Make a specified participation contribution.

BETWEEN-SHOW PROMOTIONS

Between Commerce sponsored exhibitions, U.S. Trade Centers are available to American firms wishing to display, market and sell their equipment and services or to hold training programs or seminars. Market counseling and all the Trade Center facilities are provided without charge. Two to three hundred firms annually hold such promotions.

JOINT EXPORT ESTABLISHMENT PROMOTIONS

The Joint Export Establishment Promotion (JEEP) is a type of between-show promotion especially designed to help small groups of U.S. manufacturers of related products penetrate new foreign markets under a cooperative arrangement with the Department of Commerce. The program involves a specially tailored promotion undertaken on a shared cost basis and utilizing U.S. Trade Centers in those overseas markets where research has identified sales potential for American products. Individual new-to-market firms may also arrange between-show promotions under the JEEP guidelines.

CATALOG EXHIBITIONS

U.S. firms may test product interest in foreign markets, develop sales leads, and locate agents or distributors through Commerce Department sponsored catalog exhibitions. These exhibitions feature displays of a number of American product catalogs, sales brochures and other graphic sales aids at U.S. Foreign Service posts or in conjunction with trade shows. Such exhibitions are held most extensively in developing markets where the opportunities for participation in product exhibitions are more limited. Each exhibition is supported by U.S. Foreign Service Commercial Officers as well as a U.S. industry expert selected by the Department of Commerce.

TRADE MISSIONS

U.S. businessmen can also promote sales as well as locate agents and distributors by taking part in U.S. Department of Commerce trade missions. As indicated in Chapter IV, there are two types of missions. The first is the specialized trade mission which is planned and led by the Department of Commerce. Commerce determines the product theme and itinerary on the basis of research identifying strong potential market opportunities. The second type is Industry Organized Government Approved (IOGA), which may be organized and led by state development agencies, trade associations or similar business organizations. Those meeting the criteria established by the Department of Commerce receive substantial support, including advance arrangements for a full schedule of business appointments.

IN-STORE PROMOTIONS

Foreign sales of U.S.-manufactured consumer products are best developed through in-store promotions. These Commerce sponsored events, held in foreign retail establishments, are designed to promote sales of consumer merchandise by showing the quality and variety of U.S.-made products to consumers in several selected overseas markets.

As an example of this, Commerce sponsored a large promotion of consumer goods at the Seibu Department Store chain in Tokyo in 1973. Previous to the promotion, Commerce arranged for a mission of Japanese businessmen to visit the United States and discuss with U.S. businessmen the operation of the Japanese consumer goods market and the most effective ways of entering the market.

For information on Commerce sponsored promotions overseas, contact the nearest District Office or write Office of International Marketing, U.S. Department of Commerce, Washington, D.C. 20230 or phone 202–967–2087.

XIII. MANUFACTURING OVERSEAS

Mention should be made at this point of alternate methods of selling your products overseas other than exporting. One such method is through manufacture of your product in a foreign country.

Certain products, usually consumer items, are of relatively low cost, but by the time freight and handling costs, import duties and taxes, agents' commissions, and other related costs are added, the product may be priced out of a particular foreign market. Also, the importation of some items may be prohibited. One way to overcome these barriers to export trade is by foreign manufacture.

There are three basic ways that foreign manufacturing can be accomplished: Under license to a second party; a wholly owned branch or subsidiary; or by a joint venture.

LICENSING

This method provides for rapid entry into a foreign market and is the least expensive because there is no direct investment on the part of the American firm or licensor. For these reasons it is an ideal way for smaller U.S. manufacturers to achieve a foothold in otherwise closed markets, although it is used extensively by larger firms as well.

It involves making the U.S. firm's patents and designs available to a foreign manufacturer for an established fee. Sometimes it may also include technical aid and know-how, and allow the use of the licensor's trade-mark by the licensee.

Usually the government of the host country must approve the agreement, subject to its local statutes, before it goes into effect.

Be sure to investigate not only the prospective licensee, but the country as well regarding the availability of foreign exchange, taxes, and attitude toward repatriation of royalties and dividends.

BRANCH MANUFACTURING AND SUBSIDIARY OPERATIONS

A branch manufacturing operation abroad requires a substantial investment. The U.S. firm is assured of being able to operate, subject to individual country laws, in the manner most advantageous to its international goals. It can control sales policy and production; initiate more efficient production and management methods; it offers patent and trade-mark protection, and allows it to take full advantage of any investment or tax incentives which may be offered to firms establishing new manufacturing facilities (this is especially true in some countries that grant additional relief if the product is to be exported, thus improving their balance of payments position).

Such an operation can be established by the acquisition of an existing facility or constructing a new one. Acquisition is usually the quickest and also the most economical method. An advantage to the acquisition method is obtaining the reputation and good will of the acquired firm which may be extremely important.

Again, the prospective country must be analyzed very carefully for political and economic stability, convertability of funds, taxes, etc.

It is possible to obtain investment guarantees from the U.S. Government to protect an American firm's investment in some foreign countries.

JOINT VENTURES

In other cases, to help offset the high cost of foreign investment, it is desirable to go into a joint venture with a foreign entity in the ownership of another business. An additional reason may be that the host country, by law, requires a certain percentage, often 51%, of the operation to belong to a national (citizen) of the country.

There are advantages to this method; namely, knowledge of the customs and taste of the people as well as valuable business and political contacts.

XIV. OTHER AIDS AND SERVICES YOU SHOULD KNOW ABOUT

There are many other helpful aids, services and information available to exporters both from government and private sources.

U.S. DEPARTMENT OF COMMERCE

Target Industry Program.—This unique Bureau of International Commerce program is boosting foreign sales of U.S. products by matching the most advanced and competitive U.S. industries with the best potential overseas markets for their products.

Features of the program include extensive in-depth research in the target overseas markets, a printed Global Market Survey which identifies the market potential for the industry's products in 15 to 20 countries, and development of a tailored global marketing plan for each participating company. For information on this program contact the nearest District Office or write Office of International Marketing, U.S. Department of Commerce, Washington, D.C. 20230.

The first six target industry campaigns have generated over $353 million in immediate new export business, and introduced 238 companies to exporting. A total of 15 industries have been selected for target industry treatment.

Major Projects Program.—This program, conceived in 1970 by the Bureau of International Commerce, is designed to help American companies get a bigger share of the major construction, engineering and development projects around the world.

The program is aimed at foreign contracts with an export value of $5 million or more. Direct assistance is provided to U.S. companies from the first announcement of a project still in the planning stage to actual bid. In less than 3 years, the program produced nearly $3 billion in export sales for U.S. companies.

Commerce specialists match information on each new project with American companies equipped to handle each phase of a project. These companies are notified immediately of the opportunity to bid on the project and are offered direct Commerce Department help in competing for the contract.

As an important part of this program, the Commerce Department maintains a Foreign Projects Reference Room in Room 3061 of its main building, 14th Street, N.W., between E Street and Constitution Avenue in Washington.

Here, the businessman can review a wide range of major foreign projects under consideration by international financial institutions—World Bank Group, Inter-American Development Bank, Asian Development Bank, and the United Nations Development Program.

Trade Oportunities Program.—This program also furnishes U.S. businessmen with detailed opportunities for direct sales to overseas buyers—private and government—as well as notices of foreign companies offering to represent U.S. firms overseas (See Chapter IV). American businessmen indicate the specific product categories by country for which they desire to receive sales leads or expressions of interest regarding representation, which are then added to a computerized masterfile. These businessmen, subscribing to the program, are then automatically sent related sales leads as they are telexed to the Trade Opportunity Program computer in Washington from more than 200 overseas American Embassies and Consulates.

Every lead provided to subscribing businessmen applies only to the products and information he has specified. Minimum charge for the service is $25 for 50 sales leads, although larger subscriptions are also available. For additional information, check with your nearest Department of Commerce District Office or contact the Trade Opportunities Program, U.S. Department of Commerce, Washington, D.C. 20230.

East-West Trade Assistance.—Businessmen interested in exporting to the Soviet Union, People's Republic of China (PRC) and other Eastern Europe countries can receive assistance from the newly created Bureau of East-West Trade. The Bureau is helping to develop trade with the centrally planned economies through advising individual firms on the mechanics or "how-to" of East-West trade. The Bureau fosters U.S. participation in trade fairs, exhibitions and technical seminars in these countries.

The Bureau is also conducting various market and economic studies which will provide information to the business community. One such study will indicate those products which have the best potential for export to each Eastern European country and the U.S.S.R. They will be rank-ordered on the basis of market potential. This study will be utilized by the Bureau to set promotion priorities and to establish themes for in-depth market research. Detailed market surveys are conducted by the Bureau to provide information on market potentials, competitiveness of U.S. exports, and market strategies for various products and processes. Other work includes a study on the impact and quantification of Most Favored Nation status, an analysis of PRC's foreign trade, sector analysis and trade projections.

Advising individual firms encompasses a wide range of personal services including whom to contact and how to make contact in the various countries. The Bureau's resources include information on the negotiating tactics likely to be encountered, contract clauses that need to be considered carefully, and sources and methods of financing trading agreements. Additionally, assistance can include Bureau follow-up on a U.S. business trade initiative through the American Embassy in the country concerned and the sitting in on negotiations between a U.S. firm and an East European purchasing organization.

For specific information on the personalized services that can be provided in East-West Trade, write to: Bureau of East-West Trade, U.S. Department of Commerce, Washington, D.C. 20230.

Business Counseling Services.—Businessmen may receive personal counseling both at the Department of Commerce in Washington, D.C., 14th and Constitution Avenue, or at any of the Department's 43 District Offices. The Business Counseling Section of the Department's Bureau of International Commerce in Washington, D.C. offers guidance, in-depth counseling on every phase of international trade, and the scheduling of appointments with appropriate officials within the Domestic and International Business Administration, as well as officials in other agencies. The Department's District Offices also provide business counseling services, identify foreign markets for products or services, suggest possible agents or distributors as well as sources of credit information, financing, insurance, and other special export assistance (See List of District Offices, Page 50).

District Export Councils.—In addition to the services of its District Offices, the Department of Commerce gives you direct contact with businessmen experienced in all phases of export trade through its District Export Councils. It has established one in every city that has a District Office.

These Councils assist in many of the courses, seminars and clinics on exporting arranged by the District Offices in cooperation with chambers of commerce, trade associations, banks, trade schools, colleges, and the Small Business Administration. The Council may also arrange for private consultation between experienced and prospective exporters.

Composed of business leaders in the field of foreign trade who serve without compensation, the Councils can help businessmen break into the export field.

TAX INCENTIVES FOR EXPORTERS

Currently there are two important provisions in the Internal Revenue Code that offer U.S. firms exporting American goods and/or services a certain tax advantage. Following is a brief outline of these provisions:

Domestic International Sales Corporation (DISC).— Public Law 92–178, effective January 1, 1972, added a new category of corporation to the Tax Code called a Domestic

International Sales Corporation (DISC), entitled to defer tax on 50% of its export income until distributed to shareholders. The tax-deferred earnings retained by the DISC may be invested in its own export business or loaned to domestic producers of export goods. Once a distribution is made, it is taxed to the shareholders as a dividend.

Basically a DISC is a domestic corporation which limits its activities almost solely to export sale, lease or rental transactions and related activities. It can operate as a principal, buying and selling for its own account, or as a commission agent. It can be an independent merchant or broker, or be a subsidiary of another firm.

To qualify for the deferral treatment, a corporation seeking DISC status must:

1. Be a domestic corporation.

2. Have at least $2,500 of paid-in capital on each day of the taxable year.

3. Have only one class of stock.

4. File a statement of election to be treated as a DISC with the Internal Revenue Service (IRS Form 4876), and demonstrate shareholder consent to such an election.

5. Have its own bank account and accounting records.

In addition, a DISC must meet the following income and assets tests:

At least 95% of its income must originate from qualified export receipts. These include income from the sale, lease or rental of goods manufactured, produced, grown, or extracted in the United States for ultimate use abroad. Also included are: gains from the sales of plant and equipment used in the firm's export business; dividends from a foreign selling subsidiary of the DISC; interest on certain obligations issued by the Export-Import Bank of the United States; and receipts for engineering and architectural services for foreign construction projects.

Ninety-five per cent (95%) of the DISC's assets must be

export related, i.e., export goods held in inventory; assets used in the sale, lease, rental, storage, handling, transportation, packaging, assembly, or servicing of exports, or the performance of services producing qualified export receipts; accounts receivable arising from qualified export activities; bank deposits needed to meet working capital requirements; stock or securities in a related foreign export corporation; and certain loans by the DISC to its parent or an unrelated firm for investment in export production facilities or research and development activities.

Western Hemisphere Trading Corporation (WHTC).— In 1942, legislation was passed for the purpose of placing U.S. companies doing business in the Western Hemisphere in a more competitive position with foreign firms. A company qualifying as a WHTC receives special deduction from taxable income which results in an appreciable tax reduction; i.e., it is taxed on only about 70% of its profits. In effect, a WHTC pays only 15.6% on its first $35,000 of net profit and 34% on the excess, whereas a standard domestic corporation ordinarily pays 22% tax on the first $25,000 profit and 48% on the excess.

In order to qualify, the following should be observed:

All business conducted by the WHTC must be within the Western Hemisphere (including Canada.)

Ninety-five per cent (95%) of the WHTC's income must be derived from sources outside the United States.

Ninety per cent (90%) of the gross income must be derived from the active conduct of a trade or business rather than passive means such as interest, dividends, royalties, etc.

The transfer of title to merchandise should take place outside the United States, preferably in the country of destination.

Note: The preceding is not to be construed as a complete outline of regulations which a firm must observe to qualify as a DISC or WHTC, but instead, points out only the major provisions of each. Qualified legal counsel should be contacted for assistance in establishing a DISC and/or WHTC.

CARNETS

The United States is a member of the ATA Carnet System which permits U.S. commercial and professional travelers to take commercial samples, advertising material, cinematographic, audio-visual, medical, scientific, or other professional equipment into member countries for temporary periods of time without the necessity of paying customs duty and taxes or posting a bond at the border of each country to be visited. More than 30 countries participate in the carnet system including all of Western Europe, Japan, Canada, and certain countries in Eastern Europe and Africa. Applications for carnets are made to the U.S. Council of the International Chamber of Commerce, 1212 Avenue of the Americas, New York, New York 10036. A fee is charged for the carnet depending on the value of the goods to be covered and a letter of credit or bank guaranty of 40% of the value of the goods is also required to cover duties and taxes which would be due if goods imported into a foreign country by carnet are not re-exported and the duties not paid by the carnet holder. The carnets are generally valid for a period of 12 months, although those covering professional equipment are limited by international convention to a 6-month life.

FREE PORTS AND FREE TRADE ZONES

To encourage and facilitate international trade, more than 100 free ports, free trade zones, or similar customs-privileged facilities are now in operation in some 40 countries, usually in or near seaports. Many American manufacturers or their distributors utilize free ports or free trade zones for receipt of shipments of goods which are then reshipped in smaller lots to customers throughout the surrounding area.

Information about free trade zones, free ports, and similar customs-privileged facilities abroad may be obtained from the Transportation and Insurance Division, U.S. Department of Commerce, Washington, D.C. 20230.

Exporters should also consider the customs privileges of U.S. foreign-trade zones, which make a domestic site, considered outside customs territory, available for activities that might otherwise be carried on overseas for customs reasons. For purely export operations, zones provide accelerated export status for purposes of excise taxe rebates and customs drawback. On the import and re-export side, no duties are charged on foreign goods moved into zones unless and until the goods or their products are moved into customs territory. This means that the use of zones can be considered for operations involving foreign dutiable materials and components being assembled or produced here for re-export. Also, in such cases no quota restrictions would ordinarily apply.

There are now 12 approved foreign-trade zones in the United States, located in New York, New Orleans, San Francisco, Seattle, Toledo, Mayaguez (Puerto Rico), Honolulu, McAllen (Texas), Bay City (Michigan), Little Rock, Kansas City, and Sault Ste. Marie (Michigan). The facilities are available for operations involving storage, repacking, inspection, exhibition, assembly, manufacturing, and other processing.

Over 1,223 business firms used the services of foreign-trade zones in fiscal 1972, including 115 that occupied zone facilities on a permanent basis. The value of merchandise moved to and from the zones during the year exceeded $212 million in fiscal 1972.

Information about the zones is available from each zone manager, from the Executive Secretary of the Foreign-Trade Zones Board, Department of Commerce, Washington, D.C. 20230, or from your nearest Department of Commerce District Office.

OTHER SOURCES OF AIDS, SERVICES AND INFORMATION

Other valuable sources of exporting aids, services and information include the following:
Local Chambers of Commerce
International banking departments of local banks
Chamber of Commerce of the United States
Freight Forwarders
Transportation firms (shipping companies, airlines, etc.)
Foreign Governments
Export Management Companies
Trade Associations, domestic and foreign

EXPORT REFERENCE PUBLICATIONS

GOVERNMENT

U.S. Department of Commerce
Business Service Checklist. Weekly. Lists news releases, books, pamphlets, reports, and other materials of interest to industry and business which are published by the Department of Commerce. *$7.20 a year.* Order from the Superintendent of Documents, Washington, D.C. 20402.

Checklist of International Business Publications. Lists all international publications issued by the Department of

Commerce. *Free.* Order from the National Technical Information Service, Springfield, Va. 22151.

Commerce Business Daily. A daily synopsis of U.S. Government procurement invitations, subcontracting leads, contract awards, sales of surplus property, and foreign business opportunities. Daily. Order from Department of Commerce District Offices or the Superintendent of Documents, Washington, D.C. 20402. *$63.50 a year; $120.30 airmail.*

Commerce Today. Biweekly. Principal Commerce Department publication for presenting domestic and international business news and news of the application of technology to business and industrial problems. Commerce Today succeeds International Commerce magazine and incorporates its international trade and investment news as well as material from the other business related areas of the Department. *$29.80 a year, $7.45 additional for foreign mailing, $5.75 additional for domestic airmail. Single copy $1.15.* Order from the Superintendent of Documents, Washington, D.C. 20402.

A Guide to Financing Exports. A summary of sources of credit and credit information for exports. Reviews services offered by Export-Import Bank of the United States, Foreign Credit Insurance Association, Overseas Private Investment Corporation and Commodity Credit Corporation. *Free.* Order from Office of Export Development, Department of Commerce, Room 4002, Washington, D.C. 20230.

Foreign Economic Trends and Their Implications for the United States. This series of commercial reports from Foreign Service Posts abroad presents current business and economic developments in every country that offers a present or potential market for U.S. goods. *100 to 150 reports a year, $37.50 a year.* Order from the Superintendent of Documents, Washington, D.C. 20402.

Ocean Freight Rate Guidelines. Discusses for the exporter factors he should consider in shipping his goods by ocean vessel. *75 cents.* Order from Superintendent of Documents, Washington, D.C. 20402.

Market Share Reports. Provide basic data needed by exporters to evaluate overall trends in the size of markets for manufacturers; measure changes in the import demand for specific products; compare the competitive position of United States and foreign exporters; select distribution centers for United States products abroad; and identify existing and potential markets for U.S. components, parts and accessories. *Reports for over 73 countries, $3 each. 1,100 commodity reports at $3 for one to five reports.* Order from the Superintendent of Documents, Washington, D.C. 20402.

Overseas Business Reports. Provide basic background data on specific countries. Each OBR discusses separate topics on a single country, such as basic economic data, foreign trade regulations, market factors, selling in, establishing a business, etc. 75 to 80 reports per year, *$28.50 per year.* Order from the Superintendent of Documents, Washington, D.C. 20402.

How to Get the Most From Overseas Exhibitions. Details the steps a firm should take in participating in an overeas exhibition. Contains helpful hints in planning participation. *Free.* Order from Office of Export Development, Department of Commerce, Room 4002, Washington, D.C. 20230.

Overseas Trade Promotions Calendar. Designed to help U.S. business firms take advantage of sales opportunities in overseas markets, booklet contains a 12-month schedule of U.S. Trade Center exhibitions, international trade fairs in which United States participation is planned, and a number of other overseas promotional activities planned and organized by the U.S. Department of Commerce. Revised periodically. *Free.* Order from Office of Export Development, Department of Commerce, Room 4002, Washington, D.C. 20230.

U.S. Trade Promotion Facilities Abroad. Gives detailed

description of U.S. Trade Centers overseas and includes technical data, location map photos, summaries of markets, and review of various services and programs offered by the Trade Centers. *Free.* Order from Office of Export Development, Department of Commerce, Room 4002, Washington, D.C. 20230.

The EMC—Your Export Department. Describes the services provided to exporters by Export Management Companies as well as how to go about selecting a suitable EMC. *Free.* Order from Office of Export Development, Department of Commerce, Room 4002, Washington, D.C. 20230.

Foreign Business Practices. Provides basic information on some of the laws and practices governing exporting, licensing, and investment abroad. *60¢.* Order from National Technical Information Service, Springfield, Va. 22151.

OTHER GOVERNMENT

An Introduction to the Overseas Private Investment Corporation (OPIC). Reviews how OPIC can assist U.S. firms interested in investment in developing nations. Available from Overseas Private Investment Corporation, Washington, D.C., 20527. *Free.*

Export-Import Bank of the United States. Explains United States export financing programs. Available from Export-Import Bank of the United States, 811 Vermont Avenue, N.W., Washington, D.C., 20571. *Free.*

Export Marketing for Smaller Firms. Describes how smaller business firms can either enter the export market or expand their export trade. Order from Superintendent of Documents, Washington, D.C. 20402. *60¢.*

DISC—A Handbook for Exporters. Explains how Domestic International Sales Corporation (DISC) operate, how they can be set up and their advantages for exporters. Answers basic questions about DISCs. Produced by the Treasury Department and available from Superintendent of Documents, Washington, D.C. 20402. *40¢.*

COMMERCIAL PUBLISHERS

General Foreign Trade

Adventures in Export. A. W. and W. C. King. Marsit Publishing Company, 7111 East "B" Street, Belleville, Illinois. *$2.50.*

Foreign Trade Handbook. The Dartnell Corporation, Chicago, Illinois. *$17.50.*

Handbook of International Marketing. A. O. Stanley. McGraw-Hill Book Company. *$17.50.*

International Marketing. John M. Hess and Philip R. Cateira, Richard D. Irwin, Homewood, Illinois. *$10.50.*

International Marketing. John Fayerweather, Prentice Hall, Englewood Cliffs, New Jersey. *$2.75 paperback.*

Marketing for the Developing Company. John Winker, Hutchinson and Company, London.

International Marketing Management. Michael J. Thomas, Houghton-Mifflin Company, Boston, Massachusetts. *$6.25 paperback.*

World Marketing—A Multinational Approach. John K. Ryans and James C. Baker, John Riley and Sons, New York, New York. *$9.95.*

Principals of World Business. Lawrence P. Dowd, incorporating the work of E. E. Pratt, Allyn & Bacon, 150 Tremont Street, Boston, Massachusetts. *$8.50.*

Export or Die. Charles J. Olson and Ray C. Ellis, The Dartnell Corporation, Chicago, Illinois. *$9.95.*

An Introduction to Doing Import and Export Business.

Chamber of Commerce of the United States, 1615 "H" Street, N.W., Washington, D.C., 20006. *$2.00*

Strategic Planning for Export Marketing. Franklin R. Root, International Textbook Company, Scranton, Pennsylvania. *$1.75.*

Specialized Publications

Carnet. United States Council of the International Chamber of Commerce, 1212 Avenue of the Americas, New York, New York, 10036. Explains what a carnet is and how it is of benefit to exporters. Contains application forms for applying for a carnet.

Exporters' Encyclopedia. Dun & Bradstreet, Inc., 99 Church Street, New York, New York, 10017. Contains import regulations and procedures required for shipping to every country in the world; information on preparing export shipments; list of world ports, steamship lines, air lines, Government agencies, and trade organizations; special sections on packing, marine insurance, export terms, and many other aspects of foreign trade. *$100 including monthly supplementary bulletins and newsletters.*

U.S. DEPARTMENT OF COMMERCE

Trade Centers

BEIRUT
U.S. Trade Center
American Embassy
Ali Reza Building
Corniche at Avenue de Paris
Beirut, Lebanon

BUENOS AIRES
U.S. Trade Center
Avenida Quintana 441
Buenos Aires, Argentina

FRANKFURT
U.S. Trade Center
Bockenheimer Landstrasse 2–4
6 Frankfurt/Main, Germany

LONDON
U.S. Trade Center
4/5 Langham Place
London, U.K.

MEXICO CITY
U.S. Trade Center
Apartado Postal
M-2805
Mexico City 1, D. F., Mexico

MILAN
U.S. Trade Center
Via Gattamelata, 5
20149 Milan, Italy

OSAKA
U.S. Trade Center
Sankei Kaikan Building
27, Umeda-Cho, Kita-Ku
Osaka, Japan

PARIS
U.S. Trade Center
123 Avenue Charles de Gaulle
92 Neuilly, France

SEOUL
U.S. Trade Center
82 Sejong Road
Seoul, Korea

SINGAPORE
U.S. Trade Center
First Floor
Yen San Building
168 Orchard Road
Singapore 9

STOCKHOLM
U.S. Trade Center
Vasagatan 11, S-101 28
Stockholm, Sweden

SYDNEY
U.S. Trade Center
P.O. Box 215
Royal Exchange
Sydney, N.S.W. 2000
Australia

TAIPEI
U.S. Trade Center
261 Nanking East Road
Taiwan Glass Co. Building
Taipei, Taiwan

TEHRAN
U.S. Trade Center
Elizabeth Boulevard
corner Attar Zadeh
Tehran, Iran

TOKYO
U.S. Trade Center
Tameike-Tokyu Building
1-14 Akasaka
1 CHOME
Minato-ku, Tokyo 107
Japan

VIENNA
U.S. East-West Trade Center
Prinz Eugenstrasse 8-10
A-1040 Vienna, Austria

WARSAW
U.S. Trade Information Office
Ulica Wiejska, 20
Warsaw, Poland

U.S. DEPARTMENT OF COMMERCE

District Offices

The Department of Commerce maintains 43 District Offices which bring the Department's services to the doorsteps of the nation's businessmen. Experienced specialists will provide you with a wealth of information and aids about international as well as domestic trade.

District Offices act as official sales agents of the Superintendent of Documents and stock a wide range of Commerce and other official Government publications relating to business. Each office maintains an extensive business reference library containing periodicals, directories, publications, and reports from official as well as private sources.

DISTRICT OFFICES

ALBUQUERQUE, NEW MEXICO 87101
    U.S. Courthouse (Room 316)
    (505) 766–2386

ANCHORAGE, ALASKA 99501
    412 Hill Building
    632 Sixth Avenue
    (907) 265–4547

ATLANTA, GEORGIA 30309
    Suite 523
    1401 Peachtree Street, N.E.
    (404) 526–6000

BALTIMORE, MARYLAND 21202
    415 U.S. Customhouse
    Gay and Lombard Streets
    (301) 962–3560

BIRMINGHAM, ALABAMA 35205
    Suite 201
    908 South 20th Street
    (205) 325–3327

BOSTON, MASSACHUSETTS 02116
    10th Floor
    441 Stuart Street
    (617) 223–2312

BUFFALO, NEW YORK 14202
    Room 910, Federal Building
    111 West Huron Street
    (716) 842–3208

CHARLESTON, SOUTH
    CAROLINA 29403
    Federal Building (Suite 631)
    334 Meeting Street
    (803) 577–4171

CHARLESTON, WEST VIRGINIA 25301
    3000 New Federal Office Building
    500 Quarrier Street
    (304) 343–6181

CHEYENNE, WYOMING 82001
    6022 O'Mahoney Federal Center
    2120 Capitol Avenue
    (307) 778–2151

CHICAGO, ILLINOIS 60603
    Room 1406
    Mid-Continental Plaza Building
    55 East Monroe Street
    (312) 353–4450

CINCINNATI, OHIO 45202
    8028 Federal Office Building
    550 Main Street
    (513) 684–2944

CLEVELAND, OHIO 44114
    Room 600
    666 Euclid Avenue
    (216) 522–4750

DALLAS, TEXAS 75202
    Room 3E7
    1100 Commerce Street
    (214) 749–1514

DENVER, COLORADO 80202
    New Custom House (Room 161)
    19th and Stout Streets
    (303) 837–3246

DES MOINES, IOWA 50309
    609 Federal Building

201 Walnut Street
(515) 284–4222

DETROIT, MICHIGAN 48226
445 Federal Building
(313) 226–3650

GREENSBORO, NORTH
  CAROLINA 27402
203 Federal Building
West Market Street
P.O. Box 1950
(919) 275–9111

HARTFORD, CONNECTICUT
  06103
FEDERAL OFFICE BUILDING
  (Room 610-B)
450 Main Street
(203) 244–3530

HONOLULU, HAWAII 96813
286 Alexander Young Building
1015 Bishop Street
(808) 546–8694

HOUSTON, TEXAS 77002
1017 Federal Office Building
201 Fannin
(713) 226–4231

JACKSONVILLE, FLORIDA 32207
Suite 129
4080 Woodcock Drive
(904) 791–2796

KANSAS CITY, MISSOURI 64106
Room 1840
601 East 12th Street
(816) 374–3141

LOS ANGELES, CALIFORNIA
  90024
11202 Federal Building
11000 Wilshire Boulevard
(213) 824–7591

MEMPHIS, TENNESSEE 38103
710 First American Bank Building
147 Jefferson Avenue
(901) 534–3214

MIAMI, FLORIDA 33130
City National Bank Building
  (Room 821)

25 West Flagler Street
(305) 350–5267

MILWAUKEE, WISCONSIN 53203
Straus Building
238 West Wisconsin Avenue
(414) 224–3473

MINNEAPOLIS, MINNESOTA
  55401
306 Federal Building
110 South Fourth Street
(612) 725–2133

NEW ORLEANS, LOUISIANA
909 Federal Office Building South
610 South Street
(504) 527–6546

NEW YORK, NEW YORK 10007
41st Floor, Federal Office Building
26 Federal Plaza, Foley Square
(212) 264–0634

NEWARK, NEW JERSEY 07102
24 Commerce Street
(201) 645–6214

PHILADELPHIA,
  PENNSYLVANIA 19106
10112 Federal Building
600 Arch Street
(215) 597–2850

PHOENIX, ARIZONA 85004
508 Greater Arizona Savings
  Building
112 North Central Avenue
(602) 261–3285

PITTSBURGH, PENNSYLVANIA
  15222
431 Federal Building
1000 Liberty Avenue
(412) 644–2850

PORTLAND, OREGON 97205
Suite 501, Pittock Block
921 S.W. Washington Street
(503) 221–3001

RENO, NEVADA 89502
2028 Federal Building
300 Booth Street
(702) 784–5203

RICHMOND, VIRGINIA 23240
   8010 Federal Building
   400 North 8th Street
   (804) 782–2246

ST. LOUIS, MISSOURI 63103
   2511 Federal Building
   1520 Market Street
   (314) 622–4243

SALT LAKE CITY, UTAH 84111
   1201 Federal Building
   125 South State Street
   (801) 524–5116

SAN FRANCISCO, CALIFORNIA
   94102
   Federal Building, Box 36013

   450 Golden Gate Avenue
   (415) 556–5860

SAN JUAN, PUERTO RICO 00902
   Room 100
   Post Office Building
   (809) 723–4640

SAVANNAH, GEORGIA 31402
   235 U.S. Courthouse & Post Office
      Building
   125–29 Bull Street
   (912) 232–4321

SEATTLE, WASHINGTON 98109
   706 Lake Union Building
   1700 Westlake Avenue North
   (206) 442–5615